C-1148 CAREER EXAMINATION SERIES

This is your
PASSBOOK for...

Building Maintenance Supervisor

Test Preparation Study Guide
Questions & Answers

COPYRIGHT NOTICE

This book is SOLELY intended for, is sold ONLY to, and its use is RESTRICTED to individual, bona fide applicants or candidates who qualify by virtue of having seriously filed applications for appropriate license, certificate, professional and/or promotional advancement, higher school matriculation, scholarship, or other legitimate requirements of education and/or governmental authorities.

This book is NOT intended for use, class instruction, tutoring, training, duplication, copying, reprinting, excerption, or adaptation, etc., by:

1) Other publishers
2) Proprietors and/or Instructors of "Coaching" and/or Preparatory Courses
3) Personnel and/or Training Divisions of commercial, industrial, and governmental organizations
4) Schools, colleges, or universities and/or their departments and staffs, including teachers and other personnel
5) Testing Agencies or Bureaus
6) Study groups which seek by the purchase of a single volume to copy and/or duplicate and/or adapt this material for use by the group as a whole without having purchased individual volumes for each of the members of the group
7) Et al.

Such persons would be in violation of appropriate Federal and State statutes.

PROVISION OF LICENSING AGREEMENTS – Recognized educational, commercial, industrial, and governmental institutions and organizations, and others legitimately engaged in educational pursuits, including training, testing, and measurement activities, may address request for a licensing agreement to the copyright owners, who will determine whether, and under what conditions, including fees and charges, the materials in this book may be used them. In other words, a licensing facility exists for the legitimate use of the material in this book on other than an individual basis. However, it is asseverated and affirmed here that the material in this book CANNOT be used without the receipt of the express permission of such a licensing agreement from the Publishers. Inquiries re licensing should be addressed to the company, attention rights and permissions department.

All rights reserved, including the right of reproduction in whole or in part, in any form or by any means, electronic or mechanical, including photocopying, recording, or by any information storage and retrieval system, without permission in writing from the Publisher.

Copyright © 2024 by
National Learning Corporation

212 Michael Drive, Syosset, NY 11791
(516) 921-8888 • www.passbooks.com
E-mail: info@passbooks.com

PUBLISHED IN THE UNITED STATES OF AMERICA

PASSBOOK® SERIES

THE *PASSBOOK® SERIES* has been created to prepare applicants and candidates for the ultimate academic battlefield – the examination room.

At some time in our lives, each and every one of us may be required to take an examination – for validation, matriculation, admission, qualification, registration, certification, or licensure.

Based on the assumption that every applicant or candidate has met the basic formal educational standards, has taken the required number of courses, and read the necessary texts, the *PASSBOOK® SERIES* furnishes the one special preparation which may assure passing with confidence, instead of failing with insecurity. Examination questions – together with answers – are furnished as the basic vehicle for study so that the mysteries of the examination and its compounding difficulties may be eliminated or diminished by a sure method.

This book is meant to help you pass your examination provided that you qualify and are serious in your objective.

The entire field is reviewed through the huge store of content information which is succinctly presented through a provocative and challenging approach – the question-and-answer method.

A climate of success is established by furnishing the correct answers at the end of each test.

You soon learn to recognize types of questions, forms of questions, and patterns of questioning. You may even begin to anticipate expected outcomes.

You perceive that many questions are repeated or adapted so that you can gain acute insights, which may enable you to score many sure points.

You learn how to confront new questions, or types of questions, and to attack them confidently and work out the correct answers.

You note objectives and emphases, and recognize pitfalls and dangers, so that you may make positive educational adjustments.

Moreover, you are kept fully informed in relation to new concepts, methods, practices, and directions in the field.

You discover that you are actually taking the examination all the time: you are preparing for the examination by "taking" an examination, not by reading extraneous and/or supererogatory textbooks.

In short, this PASSBOOK®, used directedly, should be an important factor in helping you to pass your test.

BUILDING MAINTENANCE SUPERVISOR

DUTIES:
A Building Maintenance Supervisor is responsible for ensuring that building and grounds maintenance and repair activities for one or more buildings in an agency are performed. The incumbent is typically responsible for supervision of a unit and may also work alongside lower-level employees in carrying out and overseeing work details. The incumbent also performs manual labor and operates equipment related to the work. The work is performed under the general direction of a superior allowing wide leeway for the exercise of independent judgment in keeping buildings and facilities up to approved standards of cleanliness and operation. Immediate supervision is exercised over the work of maintenance personnel. As a Building Maintenance Supervisor, you would direct and coordinate building and fixture maintenance and repair activities in an institution or public building and supervise the maintenance, repair, operation, construction and reconstruction of buildings and equipment at all facilities within a division including the electrical, mechanical, heating, ventilating, air conditioning and water and wastewater treatment systems. You would plan and estimate major repair and construction projects including materials and work schedules. Perform related duties as required.

DISTINGUISHING FEATURES OF THE CLASS:
The Building Maintenance Supervisor is responsible for directing the activities of the Maintenance Department. The incumbent also has oversight over the Central Services Department. The incumbent assists in the planning, assignment, and coordination of a variety of administrative and technical projects regarding the maintenance and upkeep of County buildings and grounds. The work is completed at the executive level under the general supervision of the Board of Supervisors. The position requires interaction with co-workers, engineers, architects, contractors, vendors, and the general public. The position exercises direct and functional supervision over subordinate department employees and part-time employees. The incumbent does related work as required.

SUBJECTS OF EXAMINATION:
The written test is designed to evaluate knowledge, skills, and/or abilities in the following areas:
1. **Building Maintenance and Repair**: These questions test for knowledge of the basic principles, practices and techniques essential to the proper maintenance and repair of various types of buildings, includes such areas as building maintenance, preventive maintenance, and minor repair of building structures, electrical, and plumbing systems. This may include maintenance and repair of roofs, windows, walls, floors, millwork, insulation, masonry, pipes and valves, electrical wiring and switches, and painting. Questions may also include topics such as the proper tools and materials used in building maintenance and repair work as well as proper and safe practices and techniques when using these tools and materials.
2. **Building Trades, including Mechanical and Electrical** -These questions test for knowledge of the principles and practices involved in overseeing physical plant facilities and may include such areas as maintenance and repair activities involving carpentry, electrical systems, plumbing and sanitary systems, heating and ventilating systems, painting, masonry work, roofing, and similar types of physical plant maintenance and upkeep.

3. **Review and interpretation of plans and specifications, the preparation of estimates, and oversight of contract compliance** - These questions test for ability to read and interpret building and mechanical electrical system blueprints and diagrams, to calculate material or labor cost estimates, and to read and interpret construction specifications and construction contract provisions.
4. **Operation and Maintenance of Heating, Ventilating and Air Conditioning Systems** - These questions test for knowledge of basic principles, practices and techniques essential to the correct operation and maintenance of heating, ventilating and air conditioning systems, including such areas as air supply and exhaust systems, circulating fan capacities, building ventilation requirements, steam, hot water, and hot air heating systems; boiler operation; the refrigeration cycle, types and characteristics of refrigerants, troubleshooting air conditioning system problems, and proper maintenance of air conditioning systems.
5. **Work scheduling** - These questions are designed to test how well candidates can schedule personnel for work assignments. Candidates will be provided with instructions and background information needed.
6. **Supervision** - These questions test for knowledge of the principles and practices employed in planning, organizing, and controlling the activities of a work unit toward predetermined objectives. The concepts covered, usually in a situational question format, include such topics as assigning and reviewing work; evaluating performance; maintaining work standards; motivating and developing subordinates; implementing procedural change; increasing efficiency; and dealing with problems of absenteeism, morale, and discipline.

HOW TO TAKE A TEST

I. YOU MUST PASS AN EXAMINATION

A. *WHAT EVERY CANDIDATE SHOULD KNOW*

Examination applicants often ask us for help in preparing for the written test. What can I study in advance? What kinds of questions will be asked? How will the test be given? How will the papers be graded?

As an applicant for a civil service examination, you may be wondering about some of these things. Our purpose here is to suggest effective methods of advance study and to describe civil service examinations.

Your chances for success on this examination can be increased if you know how to prepare. Those "pre-examination jitters" can be reduced if you know what to expect. You can even experience an adventure in good citizenship if you know why civil service exams are given.

B. *WHY ARE CIVIL SERVICE EXAMINATIONS GIVEN?*

Civil service examinations are important to you in two ways. As a citizen, you want public jobs filled by employees who know how to do their work. As a job seeker, you want a fair chance to compete for that job on an equal footing with other candidates. The best-known means of accomplishing this two-fold goal is the competitive examination.

Exams are widely publicized throughout the nation. They may be administered for jobs in federal, state, city, municipal, town or village governments or agencies.

Any citizen may apply, with some limitations, such as the age or residence of applicants. Your experience and education may be reviewed to see whether you meet the requirements for the particular examination. When these requirements exist, they are reasonable and applied consistently to all applicants. Thus, a competitive examination may cause you some uneasiness now, but it is your privilege and safeguard.

C. *HOW ARE CIVIL SERVICE EXAMS DEVELOPED?*

Examinations are carefully written by trained technicians who are specialists in the field known as "psychological measurement," in consultation with recognized authorities in the field of work that the test will cover. These experts recommend the subject matter areas or skills to be tested; only those knowledges or skills important to your success on the job are included. The most reliable books and source materials available are used as references. Together, the experts and technicians judge the difficulty level of the questions.

Test technicians know how to phrase questions so that the problem is clearly stated. Their ethics do not permit "trick" or "catch" questions. Questions may have been tried out on sample groups, or subjected to statistical analysis, to determine their usefulness.

Written tests are often used in combination with performance tests, ratings of training and experience, and oral interviews. All of these measures combine to form the best-known means of finding the right person for the right job.

II. HOW TO PASS THE WRITTEN TEST

A. NATURE OF THE EXAMINATION

To prepare intelligently for civil service examinations, you should know how they differ from school examinations you have taken. In school you were assigned certain definite pages to read or subjects to cover. The examination questions were quite detailed and usually emphasized memory. Civil service exams, on the other hand, try to discover your present ability to perform the duties of a position, plus your potentiality to learn these duties. In other words, a civil service exam attempts to predict how successful you will be. Questions cover such a broad area that they cannot be as minute and detailed as school exam questions.

In the public service similar kinds of work, or positions, are grouped together in one "class." This process is known as *position-classification*. All the positions in a class are paid according to the salary range for that class. One class title covers all of these positions, and they are all tested by the same examination.

B. FOUR BASIC STEPS

1) Study the announcement

How, then, can you know what subjects to study? Our best answer is: "Learn as much as possible about the class of positions for which you've applied." The exam will test the knowledge, skills and abilities needed to do the work.

Your most valuable source of information about the position you want is the official exam announcement. This announcement lists the training and experience qualifications. Check these standards and apply only if you come reasonably close to meeting them.

The brief description of the position in the examination announcement offers some clues to the subjects which will be tested. Think about the job itself. Review the duties in your mind. Can you perform them, or are there some in which you are rusty? Fill in the blank spots in your preparation.

Many jurisdictions preview the written test in the exam announcement by including a section called "Knowledge and Abilities Required," "Scope of the Examination," or some similar heading. Here you will find out specifically what fields will be tested.

2) Review your own background

Once you learn in general what the position is all about, and what you need to know to do the work, ask yourself which subjects you already know fairly well and which need improvement. You may wonder whether to concentrate on improving your strong areas or on building some background in your fields of weakness. When the announcement has specified "some knowledge" or "considerable knowledge," or has used adjectives like "beginning principles of…" or "advanced … methods," you can get a clue as to the number and difficulty of questions to be asked in any given field. More questions, and hence broader coverage, would be included for those subjects which are more important in the work. Now weigh your strengths and weaknesses against the job requirements and prepare accordingly.

3) Determine the level of the position

Another way to tell how intensively you should prepare is to understand the level of the job for which you are applying. Is it the entering level? In other words, is this the position in which beginners in a field of work are hired? Or is it an intermediate or advanced level? Sometimes this is indicated by such words as "Junior" or "Senior" in the class title. Other jurisdictions use Roman numerals to designate the level – Clerk I, Clerk II, for example. The word "Supervisor" sometimes appears in the title. If the level is not indicated by the title, check the description of duties. Will you be working under very close supervision, or will you have responsibility for independent decisions in this work?

4) Choose appropriate study materials

Now that you know the subjects to be examined and the relative amount of each subject to be covered, you can choose suitable study materials. For beginning level jobs, or even advanced ones, if you have a pronounced weakness in some aspect of your training, read a modern, standard textbook in that field. Be sure it is up to date and has general coverage. Such books are normally available at your library, and the librarian will be glad to help you locate one. For entry-level positions, questions of appropriate difficulty are chosen – neither highly advanced questions, nor those too simple. Such questions require careful thought but not advanced training.

If the position for which you are applying is technical or advanced, you will read more advanced, specialized material. If you are already familiar with the basic principles of your field, elementary textbooks would waste your time. Concentrate on advanced textbooks and technical periodicals. Think through the concepts and review difficult problems in your field.

These are all general sources. You can get more ideas on your own initiative, following these leads. For example, training manuals and publications of the government agency which employs workers in your field can be useful, particularly for technical and professional positions. A letter or visit to the government department involved may result in more specific study suggestions, and certainly will provide you with a more definite idea of the exact nature of the position you are seeking.

III. KINDS OF TESTS

Tests are used for purposes other than measuring knowledge and ability to perform specified duties. For some positions, it is equally important to test ability to make adjustments to new situations or to profit from training. In others, basic mental abilities not dependent on information are essential. Questions which test these things may not appear as pertinent to the duties of the position as those which test for knowledge and information. Yet they are often highly important parts of a fair examination. For very general questions, it is almost impossible to help you direct your study efforts. What we can do is to point out some of the more common of these general abilities needed in public service positions and describe some typical questions.

1) General information

Broad, general information has been found useful for predicting job success in some kinds of work. This is tested in a variety of ways, from vocabulary lists to questions about current events. Basic background in some field of work, such as sociology or economics, may be sampled in a group of questions. Often these are principles which have become familiar to most persons through exposure rather than through formal training. It is difficult to advise you how to study for these questions; being alert to the world around you is our best suggestion.

2) Verbal ability

An example of an ability needed in many positions is verbal or language ability. Verbal ability is, in brief, the ability to use and understand words. Vocabulary and grammar tests are typical measures of this ability. Reading comprehension or paragraph interpretation questions are common in many kinds of civil service tests. You are given a paragraph of written material and asked to find its central meaning.

3) Numerical ability

Number skills can be tested by the familiar arithmetic problem, by checking paired lists of numbers to see which are alike and which are different, or by interpreting charts and graphs. In the latter test, a graph may be printed in the test booklet which you are asked to use as the basis for answering questions.

4) Observation

A popular test for law-enforcement positions is the observation test. A picture is shown to you for several minutes, then taken away. Questions about the picture test your ability to observe both details and larger elements.

5) Following directions

In many positions in the public service, the employee must be able to carry out written instructions dependably and accurately. You may be given a chart with several columns, each column listing a variety of information. The questions require you to carry out directions involving the information given in the chart.

6) Skills and aptitudes

Performance tests effectively measure some manual skills and aptitudes. When the skill is one in which you are trained, such as typing or shorthand, you can practice. These tests are often very much like those given in business school or high school courses. For many of the other skills and aptitudes, however, no short-time preparation can be made. Skills and abilities natural to you or that you have developed throughout your lifetime are being tested.

Many of the general questions just described provide all the data needed to answer the questions and ask you to use your reasoning ability to find the answers. Your best preparation for these tests, as well as for tests of facts and ideas, is to be at your physical and mental best. You, no doubt, have your own methods of getting into an exam-taking mood and keeping "in shape." The next section lists some ideas on this subject.

IV. KINDS OF QUESTIONS

Only rarely is the "essay" question, which you answer in narrative form, used in civil service tests. Civil service tests are usually of the short-answer type. Full instructions for answering these questions will be given to you at the examination. But in case this is your first experience with short-answer questions and separate answer sheets, here is what you need to know:

1) Multiple-choice Questions

Most popular of the short-answer questions is the "multiple choice" or "best answer" question. It can be used, for example, to test for factual knowledge, ability to solve problems or judgment in meeting situations found at work.

A multiple-choice question is normally one of three types—
- It can begin with an incomplete statement followed by several possible endings. You are to find the one ending which *best* completes the statement, although some of the others may not be entirely wrong.
- It can also be a complete statement in the form of a question which is answered by choosing one of the statements listed.

- It can be in the form of a problem – again you select the best answer.

Here is an example of a multiple-choice question with a discussion which should give you some clues as to the method for choosing the right answer:

When an employee has a complaint about his assignment, the action which will *best* help him overcome his difficulty is to
- A. discuss his difficulty with his coworkers
- B. take the problem to the head of the organization
- C. take the problem to the person who gave him the assignment
- D. say nothing to anyone about his complaint

In answering this question, you should study each of the choices to find which is best. Consider choice "A" – Certainly an employee may discuss his complaint with fellow employees, but no change or improvement can result, and the complaint remains unresolved. Choice "B" is a poor choice since the head of the organization probably does not know what assignment you have been given, and taking your problem to him is known as "going over the head" of the supervisor. The supervisor, or person who made the assignment, is the person who can clarify it or correct any injustice. Choice "C" is, therefore, correct. To say nothing, as in choice "D," is unwise. Supervisors have and interest in knowing the problems employees are facing, and the employee is seeking a solution to his problem.

2) True/False Questions

The "true/false" or "right/wrong" form of question is sometimes used. Here a complete statement is given. Your job is to decide whether the statement is right or wrong.

SAMPLE: A roaming cell-phone call to a nearby city costs less than a non-roaming call to a distant city.

This statement is wrong, or false, since roaming calls are more expensive.

This is not a complete list of all possible question forms, although most of the others are variations of these common types. You will always get complete directions for answering questions. Be sure you understand *how* to mark your answers – ask questions until you do.

V. RECORDING YOUR ANSWERS

Computer terminals are used more and more today for many different kinds of exams.

For an examination with very few applicants, you may be told to record your answers in the test booklet itself. Separate answer sheets are much more common. If this separate answer sheet is to be scored by machine – and this is often the case – it is highly important that you mark your answers correctly in order to get credit.

An electronic scoring machine is often used in civil service offices because of the speed with which papers can be scored. Machine-scored answer sheets must be marked with a pencil, which will be given to you. This pencil has a high graphite content which responds to the electronic scoring machine. As a matter of fact, stray dots may register as answers, so do not let your pencil rest on the answer sheet while you are pondering the correct answer. Also, if your pencil lead breaks or is otherwise defective, ask for another.

Since the answer sheet will be dropped in a slot in the scoring machine, be careful not to bend the corners or get the paper crumpled.

The answer sheet normally has five vertical columns of numbers, with 30 numbers to a column. These numbers correspond to the question numbers in your test booklet. After each number, going across the page are four or five pairs of dotted lines. These short dotted lines have small letters or numbers above them. The first two pairs may also have a "T" or "F" above the letters. This indicates that the first two pairs only are to be used if the questions are of the true-false type. If the questions are multiple choice, disregard the "T" and "F" and pay attention only to the small letters or numbers.

Answer your questions in the manner of the sample that follows:

32. The largest city in the United States is
    A. Washington, D.C.
    B. New York City
    C. Chicago
    D. Detroit
    E. San Francisco

1) Choose the answer you think is best. (New York City is the largest, so "B" is correct.)
2) Find the row of dotted lines numbered the same as the question you are answering. (Find row number 32)
3) Find the pair of dotted lines corresponding to the answer. (Find the pair of lines under the mark "B.")
4) Make a solid black mark between the dotted lines.

VI. BEFORE THE TEST

Common sense will help you find procedures to follow to get ready for an examination. Too many of us, however, overlook these sensible measures. Indeed, nervousness and fatigue have been found to be the most serious reasons why applicants fail to do their best on civil service tests. Here is a list of reminders:

- Begin your preparation early – Don't wait until the last minute to go scurrying around for books and materials or to find out what the position is all about.
- Prepare continuously – An hour a night for a week is better than an all-night cram session. This has been definitely established. What is more, a night a week for a month will return better dividends than crowding your study into a shorter period of time.
- Locate the place of the exam – You have been sent a notice telling you when and where to report for the examination. If the location is in a different town or otherwise unfamiliar to you, it would be well to inquire the best route and learn something about the building.
- Relax the night before the test – Allow your mind to rest. Do not study at all that night. Plan some mild recreation or diversion; then go to bed early and get a good night's sleep.
- Get up early enough to make a leisurely trip to the place for the test – This way unforeseen events, traffic snarls, unfamiliar buildings, etc. will not upset you.
- Dress comfortably – A written test is not a fashion show. You will be known by number and not by name, so wear something comfortable.

- Leave excess paraphernalia at home – Shopping bags and odd bundles will get in your way. You need bring only the items mentioned in the official notice you received; usually everything you need is provided. Do not bring reference books to the exam. They will only confuse those last minutes and be taken away from you when in the test room.
- Arrive somewhat ahead of time – If because of transportation schedules you must get there very early, bring a newspaper or magazine to take your mind off yourself while waiting.
- Locate the examination room – When you have found the proper room, you will be directed to the seat or part of the room where you will sit. Sometimes you are given a sheet of instructions to read while you are waiting. Do not fill out any forms until you are told to do so; just read them and be prepared.
- Relax and prepare to listen to the instructions
- If you have any physical problem that may keep you from doing your best, be sure to tell the test administrator. If you are sick or in poor health, you really cannot do your best on the exam. You can come back and take the test some other time.

VII. AT THE TEST

The day of the test is here and you have the test booklet in your hand. The temptation to get going is very strong. Caution! There is more to success than knowing the right answers. You must know how to identify your papers and understand variations in the type of short-answer question used in this particular examination. Follow these suggestions for maximum results from your efforts:

1) Cooperate with the monitor

The test administrator has a duty to create a situation in which you can be as much at ease as possible. He will give instructions, tell you when to begin, check to see that you are marking your answer sheet correctly, and so on. He is not there to guard you, although he will see that your competitors do not take unfair advantage. He wants to help you do your best.

2) Listen to all instructions

Don't jump the gun! Wait until you understand all directions. In most civil service tests you get more time than you need to answer the questions. So don't be in a hurry. Read each word of instructions until you clearly understand the meaning. Study the examples, listen to all announcements and follow directions. Ask questions if you do not understand what to do.

3) Identify your papers

Civil service exams are usually identified by number only. You will be assigned a number; you must not put your name on your test papers. Be sure to copy your number correctly. Since more than one exam may be given, copy your exact examination title.

4) Plan your time

Unless you are told that a test is a "speed" or "rate of work" test, speed itself is usually not important. Time enough to answer all the questions will be provided, but this does not mean that you have all day. An overall time limit has been set. Divide the total time (in minutes) by the number of questions to determine the approximate time you have for each question.

5) Do not linger over difficult questions

If you come across a difficult question, mark it with a paper clip (useful to have along) and come back to it when you have been through the booklet. One caution if you do this – be sure to skip a number on your answer sheet as well. Check often to be sure that you have not lost your place and that you are marking in the row numbered the same as the question you are answering.

6) Read the questions

Be sure you know what the question asks! Many capable people are unsuccessful because they failed to *read* the questions correctly.

7) Answer all questions

Unless you have been instructed that a penalty will be deducted for incorrect answers, it is better to guess than to omit a question.

8) Speed tests

It is often better NOT to guess on speed tests. It has been found that on timed tests people are tempted to spend the last few seconds before time is called in marking answers at random – without even reading them – in the hope of picking up a few extra points. To discourage this practice, the instructions may warn you that your score will be "corrected" for guessing. That is, a penalty will be applied. The incorrect answers will be deducted from the correct ones, or some other penalty formula will be used.

9) Review your answers

If you finish before time is called, go back to the questions you guessed or omitted to give them further thought. Review other answers if you have time.

10) Return your test materials

If you are ready to leave before others have finished or time is called, take ALL your materials to the monitor and leave quietly. Never take any test material with you. The monitor can discover whose papers are not complete, and taking a test booklet may be grounds for disqualification.

VIII. EXAMINATION TECHNIQUES

1) Read the general instructions carefully. These are usually printed on the first page of the exam booklet. As a rule, these instructions refer to the timing of the examination; the fact that you should not start work until the signal and must stop work at a signal, etc. If there are any *special* instructions, such as a choice of questions to be answered, make sure that you note this instruction carefully.

2) When you are ready to start work on the examination, that is as soon as the signal has been given, read the instructions to each question booklet, underline any key words or phrases, such as *least, best, outline, describe* and the like. In this way you will tend to answer as requested rather than discover on reviewing your paper that you *listed without describing*, that you selected the *worst* choice rather than the *best* choice, etc.

3) If the examination is of the objective or multiple-choice type – that is, each question will also give a series of possible answers: A, B, C or D, and you are called upon to select the best answer and write the letter next to that answer on your answer paper – it is advisable to start answering each question in turn. There may be anywhere from 50 to 100 such questions in the three or four hours allotted and you can see how much time would be taken if you read through all the questions before beginning to answer any. Furthermore, if you come across a question or group of questions which you know would be difficult to answer, it would undoubtedly affect your handling of all the other questions.

4) If the examination is of the essay type and contains but a few questions, it is a moot point as to whether you should read all the questions before starting to answer any one. Of course, if you are given a choice – say five out of seven and the like – then it is essential to read all the questions so you can eliminate the two that are most difficult. If, however, you are asked to answer all the questions, there may be danger in trying to answer the easiest one first because you may find that you will spend too much time on it. The best technique is to answer the first question, then proceed to the second, etc.

5) Time your answers. Before the exam begins, write down the time it started, then add the time allowed for the examination and write down the time it must be completed, then divide the time available somewhat as follows:
    - If 3-1/2 hours are allowed, that would be 210 minutes. If you have 80 objective-type questions, that would be an average of 2-1/2 minutes per question. Allow yourself no more than 2 minutes per question, or a total of 160 minutes, which will permit about 50 minutes to review.
    - If for the time allotment of 210 minutes there are 7 essay questions to answer, that would average about 30 minutes a question. Give yourself only 25 minutes per question so that you have about 35 minutes to review.

6) The most important instruction is to *read each question* and make sure you know what is wanted. The second most important instruction is to *time yourself properly* so that you answer every question. The third most important instruction is to *answer every question*. Guess if you have to but include something for each question. Remember that you will receive no credit for a blank and will probably receive some credit if you write something in answer to an essay question. If you guess a letter – say "B" for a multiple-choice question – you may have guessed right. If you leave a blank as an answer to a multiple-choice question, the examiners may respect your feelings but it will not add a point to your score. Some exams may penalize you for wrong answers, so in such cases *only*, you may not want to guess unless you have some basis for your answer.

7) Suggestions
    a. Objective-type questions
        1. Examine the question booklet for proper sequence of pages and questions
        2. Read all instructions carefully
        3. Skip any question which seems too difficult; return to it after all other questions have been answered
        4. Apportion your time properly; do not spend too much time on any single question or group of questions

5. Note and underline key words – *all, most, fewest, least, best, worst, same, opposite*, etc.
6. Pay particular attention to negatives
7. Note unusual option, e.g., unduly long, short, complex, different or similar in content to the body of the question
8. Observe the use of "hedging" words – *probably, may, most likely*, etc.
9. Make sure that your answer is put next to the same number as the question
10. Do not second-guess unless you have good reason to believe the second answer is definitely more correct
11. Cross out original answer if you decide another answer is more accurate; do not erase until you are ready to hand your paper in
12. Answer all questions; guess unless instructed otherwise
13. Leave time for review

   b. Essay questions
     1. Read each question carefully
     2. Determine exactly what is wanted. Underline key words or phrases.
     3. Decide on outline or paragraph answer
     4. Include many different points and elements unless asked to develop any one or two points or elements
     5. Show impartiality by giving pros and cons unless directed to select one side only
     6. Make and write down any assumptions you find necessary to answer the questions
     7. Watch your English, grammar, punctuation and choice of words
     8. Time your answers; don't crowd material

8) Answering the essay question

Most essay questions can be answered by framing the specific response around several key words or ideas. Here are a few such key words or ideas:

M's: manpower, materials, methods, money, management
P's: purpose, program, policy, plan, procedure, practice, problems, pitfalls, personnel, public relations
   a. Six basic steps in handling problems:
     1. Preliminary plan and background development
     2. Collect information, data and facts
     3. Analyze and interpret information, data and facts
     4. Analyze and develop solutions as well as make recommendations
     5. Prepare report and sell recommendations
     6. Install recommendations and follow up effectiveness

   b. Pitfalls to avoid
     1. *Taking things for granted* – A statement of the situation does not necessarily imply that each of the elements is necessarily true; for example, a complaint may be invalid and biased so that all that can be taken for granted is that a complaint has been registered

2. *Considering only one side of a situation* – Wherever possible, indicate several alternatives and then point out the reasons you selected the best one
3. *Failing to indicate follow up* – Whenever your answer indicates action on your part, make certain that you will take proper follow-up action to see how successful your recommendations, procedures or actions turn out to be
4. *Taking too long in answering any single question* – Remember to time your answers properly

IX. AFTER THE TEST

Scoring procedures differ in detail among civil service jurisdictions although the general principles are the same. Whether the papers are hand-scored or graded by machine we have described, they are nearly always graded by number. That is, the person who marks the paper knows only the number – never the name – of the applicant. Not until all the papers have been graded will they be matched with names. If other tests, such as training and experience or oral interview ratings have been given, scores will be combined. Different parts of the examination usually have different weights. For example, the written test might count 60 percent of the final grade, and a rating of training and experience 40 percent. In many jurisdictions, veterans will have a certain number of points added to their grades.

After the final grade has been determined, the names are placed in grade order and an eligible list is established. There are various methods for resolving ties between those who get the same final grade – probably the most common is to place first the name of the person whose application was received first. Job offers are made from the eligible list in the order the names appear on it. You will be notified of your grade and your rank as soon as all these computations have been made. This will be done as rapidly as possible.

People who are found to meet the requirements in the announcement are called "eligibles." Their names are put on a list of eligible candidates. An eligible's chances of getting a job depend on how high he stands on this list and how fast agencies are filling jobs from the list.

When a job is to be filled from a list of eligibles, the agency asks for the names of people on the list of eligibles for that job. When the civil service commission receives this request, it sends to the agency the names of the three people highest on this list. Or, if the job to be filled has specialized requirements, the office sends the agency the names of the top three persons who meet these requirements from the general list.

The appointing officer makes a choice from among the three people whose names were sent to him. If the selected person accepts the appointment, the names of the others are put back on the list to be considered for future openings.

That is the rule in hiring from all kinds of eligible lists, whether they are for typist, carpenter, chemist, or something else. For every vacancy, the appointing officer has his choice of any one of the top three eligibles on the list. This explains why the person whose name is on top of the list sometimes does not get an appointment when some of the persons lower on the list do. If the appointing officer chooses the second or third eligible, the No. 1 eligible does not get a job at once, but stays on the list until he is appointed or the list is terminated.

X. HOW TO PASS THE INTERVIEW TEST

The examination for which you applied requires an oral interview test. You have already taken the written test and you are now being called for the interview test – the final part of the formal examination.

You may think that it is not possible to prepare for an interview test and that there are no procedures to follow during an interview. Our purpose is to point out some things you can do in advance that will help you and some good rules to follow and pitfalls to avoid while you are being interviewed.

What is an interview supposed to test?

The written examination is designed to test the technical knowledge and competence of the candidate; the oral is designed to evaluate intangible qualities, not readily measured otherwise, and to establish a list showing the relative fitness of each candidate – as measured against his competitors – for the position sought. Scoring is not on the basis of "right" and "wrong," but on a sliding scale of values ranging from "not passable" to "outstanding." As a matter of fact, it is possible to achieve a relatively low score without a single "incorrect" answer because of evident weakness in the qualities being measured.

Occasionally, an examination may consist entirely of an oral test – either an individual or a group oral. In such cases, information is sought concerning the technical knowledges and abilities of the candidate, since there has been no written examination for this purpose. More commonly, however, an oral test is used to supplement a written examination.

Who conducts interviews?

The composition of oral boards varies among different jurisdictions. In nearly all, a representative of the personnel department serves as chairman. One of the members of the board may be a representative of the department in which the candidate would work. In some cases, "outside experts" are used, and, frequently, a businessman or some other representative of the general public is asked to serve. Labor and management or other special groups may be represented. The aim is to secure the services of experts in the appropriate field.

However the board is composed, it is a good idea (and not at all improper or unethical) to ascertain in advance of the interview who the members are and what groups they represent. When you are introduced to them, you will have some idea of their backgrounds and interests, and at least you will not stutter and stammer over their names.

What should be done before the interview?

While knowledge about the board members is useful and takes some of the surprise element out of the interview, there is other preparation which is more substantive. It *is* possible to prepare for an oral interview – in several ways:

1) Keep a copy of your application and review it carefully before the interview

This may be the only document before the oral board, and the starting point of the interview. Know what education and experience you have listed there, and the sequence and dates of all of it. Sometimes the board will ask you to review the highlights of your experience for them; you should not have to hem and haw doing it.

2) Study the class specification and the examination announcement

Usually, the oral board has one or both of these to guide them. The qualities, characteristics or knowledges required by the position sought are stated in these documents. They offer valuable clues as to the nature of the oral interview. For example, if the job involves supervisory responsibilities, the announcement will usually indicate that knowledge of modern supervisory methods and the qualifications of the candidate as a supervisor will be tested. If so, you can expect such questions, frequently in the form of a hypothetical situation which you are expected to solve. NEVER go into an oral without knowledge of the duties and responsibilities of the job you seek.

3) Think through each qualification required

Try to visualize the kind of questions you would ask if you were a board member. How well could you answer them? Try especially to appraise your own knowledge and background in each area, *measured against the job sought*, and identify any areas in which you are weak. Be critical and realistic – do not flatter yourself.

4) Do some general reading in areas in which you feel you may be weak

For example, if the job involves supervision and your past experience has NOT, some general reading in supervisory methods and practices, particularly in the field of human relations, might be useful. Do NOT study agency procedures or detailed manuals. The oral board will be testing your understanding and capacity, not your memory.

5) Get a good night's sleep and watch your general health and mental attitude

You will want a clear head at the interview. Take care of a cold or any other minor ailment, and of course, no hangovers.

What should be done on the day of the interview?

Now comes the day of the interview itself. Give yourself plenty of time to get there. Plan to arrive somewhat ahead of the scheduled time, particularly if your appointment is in the fore part of the day. If a previous candidate fails to appear, the board might be ready for you a bit early. By early afternoon an oral board is almost invariably behind schedule if there are many candidates, and you may have to wait. Take along a book or magazine to read, or your application to review, but leave any extraneous material in the waiting room when you go in for your interview. In any event, relax and compose yourself.

The matter of dress is important. The board is forming impressions about you – from your experience, your manners, your attitude, and your appearance. Give your personal appearance careful attention. Dress your best, but not your flashiest. Choose conservative, appropriate clothing, and be sure it is immaculate. This is a business interview, and your appearance should indicate that you regard it as such. Besides, being well groomed and properly dressed will help boost your confidence.

Sooner or later, someone will call your name and escort you into the interview room. *This is it.* From here on you are on your own. It is too late for any more preparation. But remember, you asked for this opportunity to prove your fitness, and you are here because your request was granted.

What happens when you go in?

The usual sequence of events will be as follows: The clerk (who is often the board stenographer) will introduce you to the chairman of the oral board, who will introduce you to the other members of the board. Acknowledge the introductions before you sit down. Do not be surprised if you find a microphone facing you or a stenotypist sitting by. Oral interviews are usually recorded in the event of an appeal or other review.

Usually the chairman of the board will open the interview by reviewing the highlights of your education and work experience from your application – primarily for the benefit of the other members of the board, as well as to get the material into the record. Do not interrupt or comment unless there is an error or significant misinterpretation; if that is the case, do not hesitate. But do not quibble about insignificant matters. Also, he will usually ask you some question about your education, experience or your present job – partly to get you to start talking and to establish the interviewing "rapport." He may start the actual questioning, or turn it over to one of the other members. Frequently, each member undertakes the questioning on a particular area, one in which he is perhaps most competent, so you can expect each member to participate in the examination. Because time is limited, you may also expect some rather abrupt switches in the direction the questioning takes, so do not be upset by it. Normally, a board member will not pursue a single line of questioning unless he discovers a particular strength or weakness.

After each member has participated, the chairman will usually ask whether any member has any further questions, then will ask you if you have anything you wish to add. Unless you are expecting this question, it may floor you. Worse, it may start you off on an extended, extemporaneous speech. The board is not usually seeking more information. The question is principally to offer you a last opportunity to present further qualifications or to indicate that you have nothing to add. So, if you feel that a significant qualification or characteristic has been overlooked, it is proper to point it out in a sentence or so. Do not compliment the board on the thoroughness of their examination – they have been sketchy, and you know it. If you wish, merely say, "No thank you, I have nothing further to add." This is a point where you can "talk yourself out" of a good impression or fail to present an important bit of information. Remember, *you close the interview yourself*.

The chairman will then say, "That is all, Mr. _____, thank you." Do not be startled; the interview is over, and quicker than you think. Thank him, gather your belongings and take your leave. Save your sigh of relief for the other side of the door.

How to put your best foot forward

Throughout this entire process, you may feel that the board individually and collectively is trying to pierce your defenses, seek out your hidden weaknesses and embarrass and confuse you. Actually, this is not true. They are obliged to make an appraisal of your qualifications for the job you are seeking, and they want to see you in your best light. Remember, they must interview all candidates and a non-cooperative candidate may become a failure in spite of their best efforts to bring out his qualifications. Here are 15 suggestions that will help you:

1) Be natural – Keep your attitude confident, not cocky

If you are not confident that you can do the job, do not expect the board to be. Do not apologize for your weaknesses, try to bring out your strong points. The board is interested in a positive, not negative, presentation. Cockiness will antagonize any board member and make him wonder if you are covering up a weakness by a false show of strength.

2) Get comfortable, but don't lounge or sprawl

Sit erectly but not stiffly. A careless posture may lead the board to conclude that you are careless in other things, or at least that you are not impressed by the importance of the occasion. Either conclusion is natural, even if incorrect. Do not fuss with your clothing, a pencil or an ashtray. Your hands may occasionally be useful to emphasize a point; do not let them become a point of distraction.

3) Do not wisecrack or make small talk

This is a serious situation, and your attitude should show that you consider it as such. Further, the time of the board is limited – they do not want to waste it, and neither should you.

4) Do not exaggerate your experience or abilities

In the first place, from information in the application or other interviews and sources, the board may know more about you than you think. Secondly, you probably will not get away with it. An experienced board is rather adept at spotting such a situation, so do not take the chance.

5) If you know a board member, do not make a point of it, yet do not hide it

Certainly you are not fooling him, and probably not the other members of the board. Do not try to take advantage of your acquaintanceship – it will probably do you little good.

6) Do not dominate the interview

Let the board do that. They will give you the clues – do not assume that you have to do all the talking. Realize that the board has a number of questions to ask you, and do not try to take up all the interview time by showing off your extensive knowledge of the answer to the first one.

7) Be attentive

You only have 20 minutes or so, and you should keep your attention at its sharpest throughout. When a member is addressing a problem or question to you, give him your undivided attention. Address your reply principally to him, but do not exclude the other board members.

8) Do not interrupt

A board member may be stating a problem for you to analyze. He will ask you a question when the time comes. Let him state the problem, and wait for the question.

9) Make sure you understand the question

Do not try to answer until you are sure what the question is. If it is not clear, restate it in your own words or ask the board member to clarify it for you. However, do not haggle about minor elements.

10) Reply promptly but not hastily

A common entry on oral board rating sheets is "candidate responded readily," or "candidate hesitated in replies." Respond as promptly and quickly as you can, but do not jump to a hasty, ill-considered answer.

11) Do not be peremptory in your answers

A brief answer is proper – but do not fire your answer back. That is a losing game from your point of view. The board member can probably ask questions much faster than you can answer them.

12) Do not try to create the answer you think the board member wants

He is interested in what kind of mind you have and how it works – not in playing games. Furthermore, he can usually spot this practice and will actually grade you down on it.

13) Do not switch sides in your reply merely to agree with a board member

Frequently, a member will take a contrary position merely to draw you out and to see if you are willing and able to defend your point of view. Do not start a debate, yet do not surrender a good position. If a position is worth taking, it is worth defending.

14) Do not be afraid to admit an error in judgment if you are shown to be wrong

The board knows that you are forced to reply without any opportunity for careful consideration. Your answer may be demonstrably wrong. If so, admit it and get on with the interview.

15) Do not dwell at length on your present job

The opening question may relate to your present assignment. Answer the question but do not go into an extended discussion. You are being examined for a *new* job, not your present one. As a matter of fact, try to phrase ALL your answers in terms of the job for which you are being examined.

Basis of Rating

Probably you will forget most of these "do's" and "don'ts" when you walk into the oral interview room. Even remembering them all will not ensure you a passing grade. Perhaps you did not have the qualifications in the first place. But remembering them will help you to put your best foot forward, without treading on the toes of the board members.

Rumor and popular opinion to the contrary notwithstanding, an oral board wants you to make the best appearance possible. They know you are under pressure – but they also want to see how you respond to it as a guide to what your reaction would be under the pressures of the job you seek. They will be influenced by the degree of poise you display, the personal traits you show and the manner in which you respond.

ABOUT THIS BOOK

This book contains tests divided into Examination Sections. Go through each test, answering every question in the margin. We have also attached a sample answer sheet at the back of the book that can be removed and used. At the end of each test look at the answer key and check your answers. On the ones you got wrong, look at the right answer choice and learn. Do not fill in the answers first. Do not memorize the questions and answers, but understand the answer and principles involved. On your test, the questions will likely be different from the samples. Questions are changed and new ones added. If you understand these past questions you should have success with any changes that arise. Tests may consist of several types of questions. We have additional books on each subject should more study be advisable or necessary for you. Finally, the more you study, the better prepared you will be. This book is intended to be the last thing you study before you walk into the examination room. Prior study of relevant texts is also recommended. NLC publishes some of these in our Fundamental Series. Knowledge and good sense are important factors in passing your exam. Good luck also helps. So now study this Passbook, absorb the material contained within and take that knowledge into the examination. Then do your best to pass that exam.

EXAMINATION SECTION

EXAMINATION SECTION
TEST 1

DIRECTIONS: Each question or incomplete statement is followed by several suggested answers or completions. Select the one that BEST answers the question or completes the statement. *PRINT THE LETTER OF THE CORRECT ANSWER IN THE SPACE AT THE RIGHT.*

1. Linseed oil is MOST commonly used to

    A. seal wooden floors
    B. polish brass fixtures
    C. thin exterior oil base paints
    D. lubricate fan bearings

    1.____

2. The APPROXIMATE number of square feet of unobstructed corridor floorspace that one cleaner can sweep in an hour is

    A. 1200   B. 2400   C. 4000   D. 6000

    2.____

3. Of the following materials, the one MOST effective in dusting office furniture is a

    A. silk cloth   B. chamois
    C. soft cotton cloth   D. counter brush

    3.____

4. Of the following materials, the one that should be used to produce the MOST resilient flooring is

    A. concrete   B. terrazzo
    C. ceramic tile   D. asphalt tile

    4.____

5. Sweeping compound is used on concrete floors MAINLY to

    A. keep the dust down
    B. polish the floor
    C. harden the floor surface
    D. indicate which part of the floor has not been swept

    5.____

6. The type of floor finish or wax that will produce an anti-slip surface on resilient floor coverings is

    A. resin-based floor finish
    B. water emulsion wax
    C. paste wax
    D. paraffin

    6.____

7. High sheen and good wearing qualities can be obtained when polishing a waxed floor by using an electric scrubbing machine equipped with

    A. nylon disks   B. soft brushes
    C. steel wool pads   D. pumice wheels

    7.____

8. Spalling of the surface of a marble floor may result if the floor is washed with

    A. a solution of trisodium phosphate   B. a soft soap solution
    C. a neutral liquid detergent solution   D. cold water

    8.____

9. When not in use, a broom should be stored

   A. resting on the floor with the handle end down
   B. resting on the floor with the bristle end down
   C. hanging by the handle from a hook
   D. lying flat on the floor

10. The one of the following items which ordinarily requires the MOST time to wash is a(n)

    A. 5 ft x 10 ft Venetian blind
    B. 4 ft fluorescent fixture
    C. incandescent fixture
    D. 5 ft x 10 ft ceramic tile floor

11. A broom that has been properly used should GENERALLY be replaced after

    A. it has been used for one month
    B. its bristles have been worn down by more than one-third of their original length
    C. it has been used for two months
    D. its bristles have been worn down by more than two-thirds of their original length

12. The floor area of a room which measures 10 ft long x 10 ft wide is _____ sq. ft.

    A. 20   B. 40   C. 100   D. 1000

13. The FIRST thing that should be checked before an oil-fired, low-pressure steam boiler is started up in the morning is the

    A. boiler water level   B. stack temperature
    C. aquastat   D. vaporstat

14. The MAIN reason for preheating number 6 fuel oil before allowing it to enter an oil burner is to

    A. increase its viscosity
    B. decrease its viscosity
    C. increase its heating value
    D. decrease its flash point

15. A house pump is used to

    A. drain basements that become flooded
    B. pump sewage from the basement to the sewer
    C. pump city water to a roof storage tank
    D. circulate domestic hot water

16. The device which shuts down an automatic rotary cup oil burner when the steam pressure reaches a preset high limit is a

    A. pressure gage   B. pressurtrol
    C. safety valve   D. low water cutoff

17. A pressure gage connected to a compressed air tank USUALLY reads in   17._____

    A. pounds   B. pounds per square inch
    C. inches of mercury   D. feet of water

18. The device which shuts off the oil burner when the water level in the boiler is too low is   18._____
    the

    A. feedwater regulator   B. low water cutoff
    C. high water alarm   D. programmer

19. The device which shuts down an oil burner when there is a flame failure is the   19._____

    A. stack switch   B. thermostat
    C. manometer   D. modutrol motor

20. The switch which is used to shut off the oil burner in case of a fire in the boiler room is   20._____
    located

    A. on the programmer cover
    B. near the boiler room entrance
    C. on the burner motor
    D. in the custodian's office

21. The MOST likely reason for a cold water faucet to continue to drip after its washer has   21._____
    been replaced is a defective

    A. handle   B. stem   C. seat   D. bib

22. In water lines, the type of valve which should always be either fully open or fully closed is   22._____
    the

    A. needle valve   B. gate valve
    C. globe valve   D. mixing valve

23. The BEST tool to use on a 1" galvanized iron pipe nipple when unscrewing the nipple   23._____
    from a coupling is a _____ wrench.

    A. crescent   B. stillson   C. monkey   D. spud

24. The BEST way to locate a leak in a natural gas pipe line is to   24._____

    A. hold a lighted match under the pipe and move it along the length of the pipe slowly
    B. hold a lighted match about two inches above the pipe and move it along the length
       of the pipe slowly
    C. coat the pipe with a soapy solution and watch for bubbles
    D. shut off the gas at the meter and then coat the pipe with a soapy solution and
       watch for bubbles

25. When comparing a 60 watt yellow bulb with a 60 watt clear bulb, it can be said that they   25._____
    BOTH

    A. give the same amount of light
    B. use the same amount of power
    C. will burn for at least 60 hours
    D. will burn for at least 60 days

26. The output capacity of an electric motor is USUALLY rated in

    A. kilowatts B. horsepower
    C. percent D. cubic feet

27. A fuse will burn out whenever it is subjected to excessive

    A. resistance B. voltage
    C. current D. capacitance

28. Of the following, the device which uses the GREATEST amount of electric power is the

    A. electric typewriter
    B. $\frac{1}{4}$ inch electric drill
    C. floor scrubbing machine
    D. oil burner ignition transformer

29. Meters which indicate the electric power consumed in a public building are read in

    A. kilowatt-hours B. volts
    C. cubic feet D. degree days

30. Tongue and groove lumber is used for

    A. desk drawers B. hardwood floors
    C. picture frames D. cabinet doors

31. When hand sawing a 1" x 4" board parallel to the grain of the wood, the BEST saw to use is the _____ saw.

    A. cross-cut B. back
    C. hack D. rip

32. The BEST tool to use to make a recess for the head of a flat-head wood screw is a(n)

    A. counterbore B. countersink
    C. auger D. nail set

33. In attaching two pieces of wood with a nut and bolt, the holes drilled should be

    A. slightly undersize in one piece, slightly oversize in the other
    B. slightly oversize in both pieces
    C. slightly undersize in both pieces
    D. drilled from opposite sides of the joint

34. The one of the following transmission devices which should be oiled MOST often is the

    A. V-belt B. roller chain
    C. rigid coupling D. clutch plate

35. A motor-generator set is USUALLY part of a(n)

    A. steam boiler B. hydraulic elevator
    C. electric elevator D. incinerator

36. The one of the following devices which MOST frequently contains hydraulic fluid is a   36.____

    A. door closer
    B. worm gear reducer
    C. foam fire extinguisher
    D. hand winch

37. A breakdown of the causes of accidental injuries by percent would show that such injuries are *most nearly* caused   37.____

    A. 100 percent by unsafe physical working conditions
    B. 100 percent by unsafe acts of people
    C. 50 percent by unsafe physical working conditions and 50 percent by unsafe acts of people
    D. 20 percent by unsafe physical working conditions and 80 percent by unsafe acts of people

38. When using an eight-foot stepladder, a worker should climb up not more than _____ rungs.   38.____

    A. 4   B. 5   C. 6   D. 7

39. A supervisor interested in the safety of his subordinates would NOT permit   39.____

    A. using a wooden rule to take measurements near electrical apparatus
    B. using a machinist's hammer to strike a chisel
    C. removing metal chips from a machine with a rag
    D. testing the heat of a soldering iron with a piece of solder

40. If a worker feels an electric shock while using a portable electric drill, he should immediately   40.____

    A. stand on a piece of scrap lumber
    B. reverse the plug in the receptacle
    C. hold onto a grounded pipe or piece of metal
    D. take the drill out of service

KEY (CORRECT ANSWERS)

1. C	11. B	21. C	31. D
2. D	12. C	22. B	32. B
3. C	13. A	23. B	33. B
4. D	14. A	24. C	34. B
5. A	15. C	25. B	35. C
6. A	16. B	26. B	36. A
7. B	17. B	27. C	37. D
8. A	18. B	28. C	38. C
9. C	19. A	29. A	39. C
10. A	20. B	30. B	40. D

TEST 2

DIRECTIONS: Each question or incomplete statement is followed by several suggested answers or completions. Select the one that BEST answers the question or completes the statement. *PRINT THE LETTER OF THE CORRECT ANSWER IN THE SPACE AT THE RIGHT.*

1. During a shortage of custodial help in a public building, the cleaning task which will probably receive LEAST attention is 1._____

   A. picking up sweepings
   B. emptying ashtrays
   C. washing walls
   D. dust-mopping offices

2. Of the following substances commonly used on floors, the MOST flammable is 2._____

   A. resin-based floor finish
   B. floor sealer
   C. water emulsion wax
   D. trisodium phosphate

3. The MOST effective method for cleaning badly soiled carpeting is 3._____

   A. wet shampooing
   B. vacuum cleaning
   C. dry shampooing
   D. wire brushing

4. Before repainting becomes necessary, a painted wall can USUALLY be washed completely 4._____

   A. only once
   B. two or three times
   C. eight to ten times
   D. sixteen to twenty times

5. The FIRST step in routine cleaning of offices at night should be 5._____

   A. sweeping floors
   B. emptying ashtrays
   C. dusting furniture
   D. damp mopping the floors

6. Among the factors pertaining to the maintenance and cleaning of a building, the one MOST likely to be under the control of the building custodian is the 6._____

   A. size of the area
   B. density of occupancy
   C. type of occupancy
   D. standards to be maintained

7. "Treated" or "dustless" sweeping of resilient-type floors requires 7._____

   A. spraying the floors with water to keep the dust down
   B. spreading sweeping compound on the floor
   C. sweeping cloths that are chemically treated with mineral oil
   D. spraying the sweeping tool with neatsfoot oil

8. A modern central vacuum cleaner system 8._____

   A. is cheaper to operate than one portable machine
   B. generally produces less suction than a portable machine
   C. conveys the dirt directly to a basement tank
   D. must be operated only in the daytime

9. Oxalic acid can be used to   9._____

    A. remove ink spots from wood
    B. clear floor drains
    C. solder copper flashing
    D. polish brass

10. The BEST material for sealing a terrazzo floor is   10._____

    A. varnish   B. a penetrating seal
    C. shellac   D. a surface seal

11. The MOST troublesome feature in cleaning public washrooms is   11._____

    A. cleaning and deodorizing the urinals
    B. washing the toilet bowls
    C. mopping the tile floors
    D. removing chewing gum from the floors

12. In order to improve its appearance, extend its life, and reduce the labor involved in dusting, wood furniture should be polished with   12._____

    A. an oil polish
    B. a water emulsion wax
    C. a silicone and spirit chemical spray
    D. clear water

13. Ringelmann charts are useful in determining   13._____

    A. interest rates
    B. smoke density
    C. standard times for cleaning operations
    D. fuel consumption

14. A fusible plug is USUALLY found in a   14._____

    A. lighting panel   B. fire door
    C. boiler wall   D. house tank

15. In an air conditioned office, MOST people would feel comfortable when the room temperature and humidity are maintained, respectively, at   15._____

    A. 75° F and 50%   B. 70° F and 30%
    C. 75° F and 20%   D. 65° F and 75%

16. The one of the following sets of conditions which will provide the MOST efficient combustion in an oil-fired low-temperature steam boiler is _____ stack temperature, _____ CO_2.   16._____

    A. 400° F, 12%   B. 500° F, 10%
    C. 600° F, 8%   D. 700° F, 6%

17. The BEST way for a building custodian to tell if the night cleaners have done their work well is to check

    A. on how much cleaning material has been used
    B. on how much waste paper was collected
    C. the building for cleanliness
    D. the floor mops to see if they are still wet

18. The one of the following which is the BEST reason for introducing a training program is that the

    A. quality of work is above standard
    B. employees are all experienced
    C. accident rate is too high
    D. tenant complaints are negligible

19. The FIRST step in training an inexperienced individual in a particular job is to

    A. put him to work and watch for mistakes
    B. put him to work and tell him to call for help if he needs it
    C. put him at ease and then find out what he knows about the work
    D. tell him to watch the least experienced worker on the job because the training is still fresh in his mind

20. As used in job analysis, the term "job breakdown" means

    A. any equipment failure
    B. any failure on the part of the worker to complete the job
    C. dividing the job into a series of steps
    D. reducing the number of workers by 50 percent

21. At times when a public building is closed to the public, the building custodian should

    A. keep all doors locked and admit no one
    B. admit only custodial employees
    C. admit anyone as long as he signs the log
    D. admit only those who have business in the building

22. When a public building is equipped for security purposes with exterior lights on or around the building, the lights should be kept lit

    A. all night except for Saturdays, Sundays, and holidays
    B. twenty-four hours a day on weekends
    C. throughout the night, every night of the week
    D. until midnight, every night of the week

23. Custodial workers are MOST liable to injury when they are engaged in

    A. sweeping floors   B. mopping floors
    C. dusting furniture   D. moving furniture

24. The BEST place to store a wooden stepladder is

    A. in a boiler room
    B. in a stairwell
    C. in a dry room
    D. outside a basement window provided that there is a locked grating overhead

25. Of the following, the BEST action for a building custodian to take when he notices that an office worker in his building has a hot plate connected to a heavily loaded electric circuit is to

    A. remove the hot plate from the office when its owner is not present
    B. demand that the office worker remove the hot plate immediately
    C. write a report to the supervisor of the office requesting corrective action
    D. ignore the situation

26. In dealing with the public, a building custodian should be

    A. indulgent   B. courteous
    C. disagreeable   D. unavailable

27. If a building custodian sees a group of people in front of his building preparing to form a picket line, he should

    A. turn on a lawn sprinkler to spray the pickets
    B. order the pickets off the sidewalk in front of the building
    C. show the pickets he is sympathetic with their complaint
    D. contact his supervisor immediately for instructions

28. When electric service in a public building is to be shut off from 10 A.M. Tuesday to 11:30 the next morning because a new electric feeder cable is being installed, the building custodian should

    A. prepare a memo to all office supervisors in the building, notifying them of the situation, and deliver a copy to each office as soon as possible
    B. prepare a notice of the impending power stoppage and post it in the lobby early Tuesday morning
    C. tell the electrical contractor to notify the tenants when he is about to shut off the power
    D. discontinue elevator service at 10 A.M. on Tuesday as an indication to the tenants that the power supply is off

29. The BEST way to remove some small pieces of broken glass from a floor is to

    A. use a brush and dustpan
    B. pick up the pieces carefully with your hands
    C. use a wet mop and a wringer
    D. sweep the pieces into the corner of the room

30. There is a two-light fixture in the room where you are working. One of the light bulbs goes out, and you need more light to work by. You should

    A. change the fuse in the fuse box
    B. have a new bulb put in
    C. call for an electrician and stop work till he comes
    D. find out what is causing the short circuit

31. While working on the job, you accidently break a window pane. No one is around, and you are able to clean up the broken pieces of glass. It would then be BEST for you to

   A. leave a note near the window that a new glass has to be put in because it was accidently broken
   B. forget about the whole thing because the window was not broken on purpose
   C. write a report to your supervisor telling him that you saw a broken window pane that has to be fixed
   D. tell your supervisor that you accidently broke the window pane while working

32. Many machines have certain safety devices for the operators. The MOST important reason for having these safety devices is to

   A. increase the amount of work that the machines can do
   B. permit repairs to be made on the machines without shutting them down
   C. help prevent accidents to people who use the machines
   D. reduce the cost of electric power needed to run the machines

Questions 33-36.

DIRECTIONS: Answer Questions 33 through 36 only according to the information given in the following passage.

MOPPING FLOORS

When mopping hardened cement floors, either painted or unpainted, a soap and water mixture should be used. This should be made by dissolving 1/2 a cup of soft soap in a pail of hot water. It is not desirable, however, under any circumstances, to use a soap and water mixture on cement floors that are not hardened. For mopping this type of floor, it is recommended that the cleaning agent be made up of 2 ounces of laundry soda mixed in a pail of water.

Soaps are not generally used on hard tile floors because slippery films may build up on the floor. It is generally recommended that these floors be mopped using a pail of hot water in which has been mixed 2 ounces of washing powder for each gallon of water. The floors should then be rinsed thoroughly.

After the mopping is finished, proper care should be taken of the mop. This is done by first cleaning the mop in clear warm water. Then it should be wrung out, after which the strands of the mop should be untangled. Finally, the mop should be hung by its handle to dry.

33. According to the above passage, you should NEVER use a soap and water mixture when mopping _____ floors.

   A. hardened cement   B. painted
   C. unhardened cement   D. unpainted

34. According to the above passage, using laundry soda mixed in a pail of water as a cleaning agent is recommended for

   A. all floors
   B. all floors except hard tile floors
   C. some cement floors
   D. linoleum floor coverings only

35. According to the above passage, the GENERALLY recommended mixture for mopping hard tile floors is   35._____

    A. 1/2 cup of soft soap for each gallon of hot water
    B. 1/2 cup of soft soap in a pail of hot water
    C. 2 ounces of washing powder in a pail of hot water
    D. 2 ounches of washing powder for each gallon of hot water

36. According to the above passage, the PROPER care of a mop after it is used includes   36._____

    A. cleaning it in clear cold water and hanging it by its handle to dry
    B. wringing it out, untangling, and drying it
    C. untangling its strands before wringing it out
    D. untangling its strands while cleaning it in clear water

Questions 37-40.

DIRECTIONS: Answer Questions 37 through 40 only according to the information given in the following passage.

ACCIDENT PREVENTION

Many accidents and injuries can be prevented if employees learn to be move careful. The wearing of shoes with thin or badly worn soles or open toes can easily lead to foot injuries from tacks, nails, and chair and desk legs. Loose or torn clothing should not be worn near moving machinery. This is especially true of neckties which can very easily become caught in the machine. You should not place objects so that they block or partly block hallways, corridors, or other passageways. Even when they are stored in the proper place, tools, supplies, and equipment should be carefully placed or piled so as not to fall, nor have anything stick out from a pile. Before cabinets, lockers or ladders are moved, the tops should be cleared of anything which might injure someone or fall off. If necessary, use a dolly to move these or other bulky objects.

Despite all efforts to avoid accidents and injuries, however, some will happen. If an employee is injured, no matter how small the injury, he should report it to his supervisor and have the injury treated. A small cut that is not attended to can easily become infected and can cause more trouble than some injuries which at first seem more serious. It never pays to take chances.

37. According to the above passage, the one statement that is NOT true is that   37._____

    A. by being more careful, employees can reduce the number of accidents that happen
    B. women should wear shoes with open toes for comfort when working
    C. supplies should be piled so that nothing is sticking out from the pile
    D. if an employee sprains his wrist at work, he should tell his supervisor about it

38. According to the above passage, you should NOT wear loose clothing when you are   38._____

    A. in a corridor   B. storing tools
    C. opening cabinets   D. near moving machinery

39. According to the above passage, before moving a ladder, you should 39.____
    A. test all the rungs
    B. get a dolly to carry the ladder at all times
    C. remove everything from the top of the ladder which might fall off
    D. remove your necktie

40. According to the above passage, an employee who gets a slight cut should 40.____
    A. have it treated to help prevent infection
    B. know that a slight cut becomes more easily infected than a big cut
    C. pay no attention to it as it can't become serious
    D. realize that it is more serious than any other type of injury

---

KEY (CORRECT ANSWERS)

1. C	11. A	21. D	31. D
2. B	12. C	22. C	32. C
3. A	13. B	23. D	33. C
4. B	14. C	24. C	34. C
5. B	15. A	25. C	35. D
6. D	16. A	26. B	36. B
7. C	17. C	27. D	37. B
8. C	18. C	28. A	38. D
9. A	19. C	29. A	39. C
10. B	20. C	30. B	40. A

TEST 3

DIRECTIONS: Each question or incomplete statement is followed by several suggested answers or completions. Select the one that BEST answers the question or completes the statement. *PRINT THE LETTER OF THE CORRECT ANSWER IN THE SPACE AT THE RIGHT.*

1. An electric motor fire should be put out with an extinguisher that uses 1.____
    - A. carbon dioxide
    - B. soda-acid
    - C. foam
    - D. a pump tank

2. The charge in a soda-acid fire extinguisher should be replaced once 2.____
    - A. a month
    - B. every three months
    - C. every six months
    - D. a year

3. An elevator machinery room should have a fire extinguisher of the _____ type. 3.____
    - A. soda-acid
    - B. foam
    - C. carbon dioxide
    - D. sand pail

4. The national flag should be raised 4.____
    - A. slowly and lowered briskly
    - B. briskly and lowered slowly
    - C. briskly and lowered briskly
    - D. slowly and lowered slowly

5. The material which is used to seal the outside edges of a pane of window glass is 5.____
    - A. stellite
    - B. putty
    - C. plastic wood
    - D. caulking compound

6. The ceiling of a room which measures 20 ft x 30 ft is to be given two coats of paint. If one gallon of paint will cover 500 square feet, the two coats of paint will require a MINIMUM of _____ gallons. 6.____
    - A. 1.5
    - B. 2
    - C. 2.4
    - D. 3.2

7. Rubbish, sticks, and papers on the lawn in front of a building should be collected by using a 7.____
    - A. rake
    - B. broom
    - C. paper sticker
    - D. hoe

8. Mortar stains on brickwork can be scrubbed off by using a solution of 8.____
    - A. benzine
    - B. tri-sodium phosphate
    - C. muriatic acid
    - D. acetic acid

9. The BEST chemical for melting ice on sidewalks is 9.____
    - A. sodium chloride
    - B. calcium carbonate
    - C. hydrogen sulphide
    - D. calcium chloride

10. Before painting a kitchen wall,

    A. a degreaser must be mixed with the paint
    B. all traces of grease must be washed off
    C. a water-base paint must be used to dissolve the grease
    D. the walls must be sanded to remove all traces of grease and old paint

11. For interior walls which must be washed very often, the PREFERRED paint is

    A. enamel   B. flat
    C. exterior varnish   D. calsomine

12. A type of window which is USUALLY equipped with sash cords or chains is the _____ type.

    A. hopper   B. awning
    C. casement   D. double-hung

13. The slats of a Venetian blind are usually tilted by a device containing a _____ gear.

    A. worm   B. spur   C. hypoid   D. bevil

14. When washing the outside of a window with a narrow inside sill, a window cleaner should place his water pail on

    A. the outside window sill
    B. the nearest desk or chair
    C. a radiator at the center of the window
    D. the floor at a convenient point toward one side of the window

15. In order to determine the carrying capacity of a passenger elevator, a custodian would have to

    A. measure the floor area
    B. check the diameter of the cable
    C. read the inspection certificate
    D. read the motor nameplate

16. Before pruning a tree, the FIRST step should be to determine

    A. if there is insect infestation
    B. the general health of the tree
    C. the desired results
    D. amount of excess foliage

17. Tree fertilizer should have a high content of

    A. slaked lime   B. chlordane
    C. rose dust   D. nitrogen

18. A gasoline-driven snow blower should be stored for the summer with its fuel tank

    A. filled with gasoline
    B. and fuel lines drained
    C. filled with water
    D. half filled with number 4 fuel oil

19. A pipe that "sweats" in the summer time PROBABLY contains 19.____

    A. hot water
    B. low pressure steam
    C. domestic gas
    D. cold water

20. A good preventive maintenance program requires that each item of equipment be 20.____

    A. represented by an up-to-date record card on file
    B. lubricated daily
    C. brand new at the start of the program
    D. painted inside and out

Questions 21-24.

DIRECTIONS: Questions 21 through 24, inclusive, are to be answered SOLELY on the basis of the following paragraph.

All cleaning agents and supplies should be kept in a central storeroom which should be kept looked and only the custodian, storekeeper and foreman should have keys. Shelving should be provided for the smaller items, while barrels containing scouring powder or other bulk material should be set on the floor or on special cradles. Each compartment in the shelves should be marked plainly and only the item indicated stored therein. Each barrel should also be marked plainly. It may also be desirable to keep special items such as electric lamps, flashlight batteries, etc., in a locked cabinet or separate room to which only the custodian and the night building foreman have keys.

21. According to the above paragraph, scouring powder 21.____

    A. should be kept on shelves
    B. comes in one-pound cans
    C. should be kept in a locked cabinet
    D. is a bulk material

22. According to the above paragraph, 22.____

    A. the storekeeper should not be entrusted with the safekeeping of light bulbs
    B. flashlight batteries should be stored in barrels
    C. the central storeroom should be kept locked
    D. only special items should be stored under lock and key

23. According to the above paragraph, 23.____

    A. each shelf compartment should contain at least four different items
    B. barrels must be stored in cradles
    C. all items stored should be in marked compartments
    D. crates of light bulbs should be stored in cradles

24. As used in the above paragraph, the word *cradle* means a 24.____

    A. dolly
    B. support
    C. doll's bed
    D. hand truck

Questions 25-28.

DIRECTIONS: Questions 25 through 28, inclusive, are to be answered SOLELY on the basis of the following paragraph.

There are on the market many cleaning agents for which amazing claims are made. Chemical analysis shows that the majority of them are well-known chemicals slightly modified and packaged and sold under various trade names. For that reason, the agents which have been selected for your use are those whose cleaning properties are well-known and whose use can be standardized. It is obviously undesirable to offer too wide a selection as that would be confusing to the cleaner, but a sufficient number must be provided so that a satisfactory agent is available for each task.

25. According to the above paragraph,

    A. there are few cleaning agents on the market
    B. there are no really good cleaning agents on the market
    C. cleaning agents are sold under several different brand names
    D. all cleaning agents are the same

26. According to the above paragraph,

    A. all cleaning agents should be chemically analyzed before use
    B. the best cleaning agents are those for which no claims are made by the manufacturer
    C. different cleaning agents may be needed for different tasks
    D. all cleaning agents have been standardized by the federal government

27. As used in the above paragraph, the word *amazing* means

    A. illegal   B. untrue
    C. astonishing   D. specific

28. As used in the above paragraph, the word *modified* means

    A. changed   B. refined   C. labelled   D. diluted

29. The MAIN reason for keeping an inventory of housekeeping supplies is to

    A. be sure that supplies are available when needed
    B. determine the cost of the supplies
    C. automatically prevent waste of the supplies
    D. be sure that at least two years' supplies are on hand at all times

30. Current daily records are MOST desirable in dealing with problems concerning

    A. accidents
    B. vandalism
    C. employee time and attendance
    D. the consumption of electricity

31. The continuous record of activities taking place in a boiler room is called a

    A. computer   B. data bank
    C. log book   D. time sheet

32. The one of the following subjects of a fire prevention training program which is MOST readily applied on the job is the

   A. elimination of fire hazards
   B. use of portable fire extinguishers
   C. knowledge of types of fires
   D. method of reporting fires

32.____

33. A good supervisor will NOT

   A. tell his men what their jobs are and why they are important
   B. show his men how their jobs are to be done in the right way
   C. require some of the men to do their jobs in the presence of the supervisor demonstrating that they understand the job
   D. leave his men alone because they will always do their jobs correctly once they have received their instructions

33.____

34. When a supervisor sees a worker doing his job incorrectly, he should

   A. tell the worker to be more careful
   B. suspend the worker until he learns to do the job correctly
   C. tell the worker specifically how the job should be done
   D. scold the man

34.____

35. An office worker complains to a custodian that one of the cleaners broke off a branch of a plant which she kept on her desk and that she can identify the cleaner.
The BEST thing for the custodian to do is to

   A. convince her that the plant will grow another branch eventually
   B. make the cleaner apologize and pay for a new plant out of his own pocket
   C. sympathize with the office worker and assure her that he will speak to the cleaner about it
   D. tell her not to bother him about her personal property

35.____

36. An employee who is a good worker but is often late for work

   A. is lazy and should be dismissed
   B. cannot tell time
   C. can have no excuse for being late more than once a month
   D. should be questioned by his supervisor to try to find out why he is late

36.____

37. When starting any disciplinary action, a good supervisor should

   A. show his annoyance by losing his temper
   B. be apologetic
   C. be sarcastic
   D. be firm and positive

37.____

38. Good public relations can be damaged by a custodian who treats tenants, fellow workers, friends, relatives, and the public with

   A. courtesy   B. consideration
   C. contempt   D. respect

38.____

39. The BEST way for a supervisor to maintain good employee morale is to

   A. avoid praising any one employee
   B. always have an alibi for his own mistakes
   C. encourage cliques by given them information before giving it to other workers
   D. give adequate credit and praise when due

40. When a new employee reports to a custodian on his first day on the job, the custodian should

   A. extend a hearty welcome and make the new employee feel welcome
   B. have the man sit and wait for a while before seeing him so that the employee realizes how busy the custodian is
   C. warn him of stern disciplinary action if he is late or absent excessively
   D. tell him he probably will have difficulty doing the work so that he doesn't become overconfident

KEY (CORRECT ANSWERS)

1. A	11. A	21. D	31. C
2. D	12. D	22. C	32. A
3. C	13. A	23. C	33. D
4. B	14. D	24. B	34. C
5. B	15. C	25. C	35. C
6. C	16. C	26. C	36. D
7. A	17. D	27. C	37. D
8. C	18. B	28. A	38. C
9. D	19. D	29. A	39. D
10. B	20. A	30. C	40. A

EXAMINATION SECTION
TEST 1

DIRECTIONS: Each question or incomplete statement is followed by several suggested answers or completions. Select the one that BEST answers the question or completes the statement. *PRINT THE LETTER OF THE CORRECT ANSWER IN THE SPACE AT THE RIGHT.*

1. As a member of a repair crew, you have been asked by your supervisor to reinforce a door. You have never done this kind of work before and are not certain how to go about it. Of the following, the MOST advisable action to take is to

    A. tell your supervisor you need assistance
    B. ask the other crew members if they can help you
    C. go ahead and do the best you can
    D. ask another member of your crew if he will do it for you

    1.____

2. It is BEST to erect a barricade or barrier before repair work begins *mainly* because

    A. the repair truck can be sent back for additional supplies
    B. the workers can work in more comfortable space
    C. unauthorized persons are kept clear of the work area
    D. a solid platform is provided for workers' use

    2.____

3. Of the following, the BEST reason for sprinkling water on work areas which have a lot of dust or where the work itself will create a lot of dust is that this action will

    A. dissolve the dust particles
    B. help the dust to settle
    C. clean away the dust from the area
    D. prevent the dust from drying out

    3.____

QUESTIONS 4-9.
Questions 4 through 9 are to be answered *solely* on the basis of the following set of instructions.

Patching Simple Cracks in a Built-Up Roof

If there is a visible crack in built-up roofing, the repair is simple and straight forward:
1. With a brush, clean all loose gravel and dust out of the crack, and clean three or four inches around all sides of it.
2. With a trowel or putty knife, fill the crack with asphalt cement and then spread a layer of asphalt cement about 1/8 inch thick over the cleaned area.
3. Place a strip of roofing felt big enough to cover the crack into the wet cement and press it down firmly.
4. Spread a second layer of cement over the strip of felt and well past its edges.
5. Brush gravel back over the patch.

4. According to the above passage, in order to patch simple cracks in a built-up roof, it is necessary to use a

    A. putty knife and a drill   B. knife and pliers
    C. tack hammer and a punch   D. brush and a trowe

    4.____

19

5. According to the above passage, the size of the area that should be clear of loose gravel and dust before the asphalt cement is first applied should

   A. be the exact size of the crack itself
   B. extend three or four inches on all sides of the crack
   C. be 1/8 inch greater than the size of the crack itself
   D. extend the length of the roofing strip

5.____

6. According to the above passage, loose gravel and dust in the crack should be removed with a

   A. brush   B. felt pad   C. trowel   D. dust mop

6.____

7. Assume that both layers of asphalt cement needed to patch the crack are of the same thickness.
   The total thickness of asphalt cement used in the patch should be, *most nearly*, _____ inch.

   A. 1/2   B. 1/3   C. 1/4   D. 1/8

7.____

8. According to the instructions in the above passage, how large should the strip of roofing felt be cut?

   A. Three of four inches square
   B. Smaller than the crack and small enough to be surrounded by cement on all sides of the strip
   C. Exactly the same size and shape of the area covered by the wet cement
   D. Large enough to completely cover the crack

8.____

9. The final or finishing action to be taken in patching a simple crack in a built-up roof is to

   A. clean out the inside of the crack
   B. spread a layer of asphalt a second time
   C. cover the crack with roofing felt
   D. cover the patch of roofing felt and cement with gravel

9.____

10. As a repair crew worker, your supervisor tells you that he has in the workshop a piece of glass measuring 5' x 4' from which he wants you to cut a section measuring 4'8" x 3'2". However, you find two pieces of glass in the workshop; one is 5' x 3', and the other is 8' x 5'.
    Of the following, the BEST action for you to take is to

    A. cut a section measuring 4'8" x 3' from the smaller piece because that is probably what he meant
    B. do NOT cut the glass and wait until he asks you for it
    C. tell him about the differences in measurement and ask him what to do
    D. cut a section measuring 4'8" x 3'2" from the larger piece since that would give you the full size required

10.____

11. A floor that is 9' wide by 12' long measures how many square feet?

    A. 12   B. 21   C. 108   D. 150

11.____

12. The sum of 5 1/16, 4 1/4, 4 3/8, and 3 7/16 is   12.____

    A. 17 1/8   B. 17 7/16   C. 17 1/4   D. 17 3/8

13. From a length of pipe 6 feet 9 inches long you are asked to cut a piece 4 feet 5 inches   13.____
    long.
    The length of the remainder, in inches, should be

    A. 24   B. 26   C. 28   D. 53

QUESTIONS 14-17.
In answering questions 14 through 17 refer to the label pictured below.

LABEL

BREGSON'S CLEAR GLUE HIGHLY FLAMMABLE	PRECAUTIONS
A clear quick-drying glue For temporary bonding, apply glue to one surface and join immediately	Use with adequate ventilation Close container after use
For permanent bonding, apply glue to both surfaces, permit to dry and press together	Keep out of reach of children
Use for bonding plastic to plastic, plastic to wood, and wood to wood only	Avoid prolonged breathing of vapors and repeated contact with skin
Will not bond at temperatures below 60°	

14. Assume that you, as a member of a repair crew, have been asked to repair a wood ban-   14.____
    ister in the hallway of a house. Since the heat has been turned off, the hallway is very
    cold, except for the location where you have to make the repair. Another repair crew
    worker is working at that same location using a blow torch to solder a pipe in the wall.
    The temperature at that location is about 67°.
    According to the instruction on the above label, the use of this glue to make the neces-
    sary repair is

    A. *advisable;* the glue will bond wood to wood
    B. *advisable;* the heat form the soldering will cause the glue to dry quickly
    C. *inadvisable;* the work area temperature is too low
    D. *inadvisable;* the glue is highly flammable

15. According to the instructions on the above label, this glue should NOT be used for which   15.____
    of the following applications?

    A. Affixing a pine table leg to a walnut table
    B. Repairing leaks around pipe joints
    C. Bonding a plastic knob to a cedar drawer
    D. Attaching a lucite knob to a lucite drawer

16. According to the instructions on the above label, using this glue to bond ceramic tile to a plaster wall by coating both surfaces with glue, letting the glue dry, and then pressing the tile to the plaster wall is

    A. *advisable;* the glue is quick drying and clear
    B. *advisable;* the glue should be permanently affixed to the one surface of the tile only
    C. *inadvisable;* the glue is not suitable for bonding ceramic tile to plaster walls
    D. *inadvisable;* the bonding should be a temporary one

17. The precaution described in the above label "use with adequate ventilation" means that

    A. the area you are working in should be very cold
    B. there should be sufficient fresh air where you are using the glue
    C. you should wear gloves to avoid contact with the glue
    D. you must apply a lot of glue to make a permanent bond

QUESTIONS 18-20.
Questions 18 through 20 are to be answered *solely* on the basis of the following passage.

A utility plan is a floor plan which shows the layout of a heating, electrical, plumbing, or other utility system. Utility plans are used primarily by the persons responsible for the utilities, but they are important to the craftsman as well. Most utility installations require the leaving of openings in walls, floors, and roofs for the admission or installation of utility features. The craftsman who is, for example, pouring a concrete foundation wall must study the utility plans to determine the number, sizes, and locations of the openings he must leave for piping, electric lines, and the like.

18. The one of the following items of information which is LEAST likely to be provided by a utility plan is the

    A. location of the joists and frame members around
    B. stairwells
    C. location of the hot water supply and return piping
    D. location of light fixtures D. number of openings in the floor for radiators

19. According to the passage, the persons who will *most likely* have the GREATEST need for the information included in a utility plan of a building are those who

    A. maintain and repair the heating system
    B. clean the premises
    C. paint housing exteriors
    D. advertise property for sale

20. According to the passage, a repair crew member should find it MOST helpful to consult a utility plan when information is needed about the

    A. thickness of all doors in the structure
    B. number of electrical outlets located throughout the structure
    C. dimensions of each window in the structure
    D. length of a roof rafter

KEY (CORRECT ANSWERS)

1. A
2. C
3. B
4. D
5. B

6. A
7. C
8. D
9. D
10. C

11. C
12. A
13. C
14. D
15. B

16. C
17. B
18. A
19. A
20. B

TEST 2

DIRECTIONS: Each question or incomplete statement is followed by several suggested answers or completions. Select the one that BEST answers the question or completes the statement. *PRINT THE LETTER OF THE CORRECT ANSWER IN THE SPACE AT THE RIGHT.*

1. Repair crew men should report accidents on the job IMMEDIATELY *primarily* so that   1.___

    A. the proper person will be reprimanded for his carelessness
    B. a correct count can be kept of time lost through accidents on the job
    C. prompt medical care may be given when needed
    D. the correct forms will be filled out

2. In a circulating hot-water heating system, most boilers have an altitude gauge that shows the level of the water in the system. This gauge has two needles, one red, which is set at the proper water level, and one black, which shows the true water level, and which varies with the water-level change. When the red needle is over the black on the gauge, so that they coincide, it means that the system   2.___

    A. has too much water
    B. requires more water
    C. is properly filled with water
    D. should be shut off

3. If a radiator fails to heat properly, the FIRST of the following actions which you should take is to check the   3.___

    A. boiler's steam gauge   B. boiler's water line
    C. radiator's shut-off valve   D. pressure reducing valve

4. Assume that you have been asked to remove a door knob. You inspect the door and find that it has a mortise lock, and that the door knob is fastened with a set screw.
Which of the following is the FIRST step that you should take in removing the door knob?   4.___

    A. Unscrew the set screw on the slimmest part of the knob
    B. Saw off the knob at its thinnest point
    C. Turn the knob repeatedly to the right and to the left until it finally falls off
    D. Use a pinchbar to spring the lock

5. When preparing a 1:1:6 mix for mortar, how many pails of lime should be added to 3 pails of sand and 1/2 pail of cement?   5.___

    A. 3   B. 1   C. 1/2   D. 1/4

6. If you find that the putty in the can is a little too hard to use, you should add some   6.___

    A. whiting   B. linseed oil
    C. spackle   D. glazing compound

7. The purpose of scratching the surface of the first coat of patching stucco is to   7.____

   A. spread the patching stucco over a wide area
   B. give the surface a textured finish
   C. provide a gripping surface for the next coat of patching stucco
   D. press the patching stucco into the hole to be repaired

8. When filling in large cracks and holes up to 2 inches in diameter in plaster walls it is BEST to use   8.____

   A. spackle   B. patching plaster
   C. gypsum wallboard   D. tile

9. Of the following, the MAIN reason for having a vertical distance of about 7 inches between stair treads is that this   9.____

   A. makes for the best appearance
   B. makes an easy step for the average person
   C. allows for the most profitable use of wood
   D. cuts out a good deal of unnecessary work

10. When removing a door from its hinges to make repairs, it is ALWAYS best to   10.____

    A. remove the pin from the top hinge first
    B. keep the door tightly closed
    C. remove the pin from the bottom hinge first
    D. remove the door knob and lock

11. Dry plaster will absorb water from the patching material, weakening and shrinking it. Based on the information in this statement, it would be *advisable* to take which one of the following actions in the process of patching a plaster crack?   11.____

    A. Mix the plaster with a lot of extra water
    B. Apply water-eased paint to the wall immediately
    C. Apply plaster powder to the crack, then pour water in over it
    D. Dampen the area surrounding the patch with a sponge

12. Standard electrical tools which are safe for ordinary use may be unsafe in locations which contain flammable materials because   12.____

    A. there may be insufficient ventilation
    B. sparks from the tools may start a fire
    C. electric current will usually cause fire
    D. the automatic sprinkler system may be set off accidentally

13. Of the following, the BEST combination of ingredients to use for good concrete is   13.____

    A. cement and water
    B. aggregate and water
    C. cement, sand, stone, and water
    D. gravel, cement, and water

14. If the blade of a screw driver is thicker than the slot at the top of a screw, the way to *properly* drive the screw into wood in this case is to

    A. widen the slot of the screw to fit the larger blade tip
    B. tap the end of the screw driver lightly to get a firmer hold into the screw slot
    C. get another screw driver which fits the size of the screw slot
    D. apply a drop of lubricating oil to the screw slot to get the screw started into the wood

QUESTIONS 15-20.
Questions 15 through 20 are to be answered *solely* on the basis of the following passage.

The basic hand-operated hoisting device is the tackle or purchase, consisting of a line called a fall, reeved through one or more blocks.

To hoist a load of given size, you must set up a rig with a safe working load equal to or in excess of the load to be hoisted. In order to do this, you must be able to calculate the safe working load of a single part of line of given size; the safe working load of a given purchase which contains a line of given size; and the minimum size of hooks or shackles which you must use in a given type of purchase to hoist a given load. You must also be able to calculate the thrust which a given load will exert on a gin pole or a set of shears inclined at a given angle; the safe working load which a spar of a given size, used as a gin pole or as one of a set of shears, will sustain; and the stress which a given load will set up in the back guy of a gin pole, or in the back guy of a set of shears, inclined at a given angle.

15. The above passage refers to the lifting of loads by means of

    A. erected scaffolds   B. manual rigging devices
    C. power-driven equipment   D. conveyor belts

16. It can be concluded from the above passage, that a set of shears serves to

    A. absorb the force and stress of the working load
    B. operate the tackle
    C. contain the working load
    D. compute the safe working load

17. According to the above passage, a spar can be used for a

    A. back guy   B. block   C. fall   D. gin pole

18. According to the above passage, the rule that a user of hand-operated tackle MUST follow is to make sure that the safe working load is at LEAST

    A. equal to the weight of the given load
    B. twice the combined weight of the block and falls
    C. one-half the weight of the given load
    D. twice the weight of the given load

19. According to the above passage, the two parts that make up a tackle are

    A. back guys and gin poles   B. blocksm and falls
    C. rigs and shears   D. spars and shackles

20. According to the above passage, in order to determine whether it is safe to hoist a particular load, you MUST

   A. use the maximum size hooks
   B. time the speed to bring a given load to a desired place
   C. calculate the forces exerted on various types of rigs
   D. repeatedly lift and lower various loads

20.____

KEY (CORRECT ANSWERS)

1.	C	11.	D
2.	C	12.	B
3.	C	13.	C
4.	A	14.	C
5.	C	15.	B
6.	B	16.	A
7.	C	17.	D
8.	B	18.	A
9.	B	19.	B
10.	C	20.	C

EXAMINATION SECTION
TEST 1

DIRECTIONS: Each question or incomplete statement is followed by several suggested answers or completions. Select the one that BEST answers the question or completes the statement. *PRINT THE LETTER OF THE CORRECT ANSWER IN THE SPACE AT THE RIGHT.*

1. Asbestos was used as a covering on electrical wires to provide protection from 1._____

    A. high voltage
    B. high temperature
    C. water damage
    D. electrolysis

2. The rating term *240 volts, 10 H.P.* would be PROPERLY used to describe a 2._____

    A. transformer
    B. storage battery
    C. motor
    D. rectifier

3. Rigid steel conduit used for the protection of electrical wiring is GENERALLY either galvanized or enameled both inside and out in order to 3._____

    A. prevent damage to the wire insulation
    B. make threading of the conduit easier
    C. prevent corrosion of the conduit
    D. make the conduit easier to handle

4. BX is COMMONLY used to indicate 4._____

    A. rigid conduit without wires
    B. flexible conduit without wires
    C. insulated wires covered with flexible steel armor
    D. insulated wires covered with a non-metallic covering

5. If a test lamp does not light when placed in series with a fuse and an appropriate battery, it is a GOOD indication that the fuse 5._____

    A. is open-circuited
    B. is short-circuited
    C. is in operating condition
    D. has zero resistance

6. Of the following, the SIMPLEST wood joint to make is a 6._____

    A. half lap joint
    B. mortise and tenon
    C. butt joint
    D. multiple dovetail

7. To accurately cut a number of lengths of wood at an angle of 45 degrees, it would be BEST to use a 7._____

    A. protractor
    B. mitre-box
    C. triangle
    D. square

8. The soffit of a beam is the 8._____

    A. span   B. side   C. bottom   D. top

9. A nail set is a tool used for

   A. straightening bent nails
   B. cutting nails to specified size
   C. sinking a nail head in wood
   D. measuring nail size

10. It is UNLAWFUL to

    A. use wooden lath
    B. have ceiling lath run in one direction only
    C. break joints when using wood lath
    D. run wood lath through from room to room

11. A concrete mix for a construction job requires a certain ratio of cement, water, sand, and small stones.
    The MOST serious error in mixing would be to use 20% too much

    A. sand
    B. water
    C. small stones
    D. mixing time

12. Impurities in a mortar which may seriously affect its strength are MOST likely to enter the mortar with the

    A. mixing water
    B. sand
    C. lime
    D. gypsum

13. One ADVANTAGE of using plywood instead of boards for concrete forms is that plywood

    A. needs no bracing
    B. does not split easily
    C. sticks less to concrete
    D. insulates concrete against freezing

14. Concrete will crack MOST easily when it is subject to

    A. compression
    B. bearing
    C. bonding
    D. tension

15. Where a smooth dense finish is desired for a concrete surface, it will BEST be produced by using a

    A. wood float
    B. level
    C. steel trowel
    D. vibrator

16. Sewer gas is prevented from backing up through a fixture by a

    A. water trap
    B. vent pipe
    C. check valve
    D. float valve

17. Packing is used in an adjustable water valve MAINLY to

    A. make it air-tight
    B. prevent mechanical wear
    C. regulate the water pressure
    D. make it water-tight

18. Good practice requires that the end of a piece of water pipe be reamed to remove the inside burr after it has been cut to length.
The PURPOSE of the reaming is to

    A. finish the pipe accurately to length
    B. make the threading easier
    C. avoid cutting of the workers' hands
    D. allow free passage for the flow of water

18.____

19. The MAIN reason for pitching a steam pipe in a heating system is to

    A. prevent accumulation of condensed steam
    B. present a smaller radiating surface
    C. facilitate repairs
    D. reduce friction in the pipe

19.____

20. When fitting pipe together, poor alignment of pipe and fittings would MOST likely result in

    A. leaky joints
    B. cracking of the pipe on expansion
    C. formation of hot spots
    D. cracking of the pipe on contraction

20.____

21. Roofing nails are GENERALLY

    A. brass plated   B. galvanized
    C. cement coated   D. nickel plated

21.____

22. Specifications for a roofing job call for 3 *lbs. sheet lead*. This means that each sheet SHOULD weigh 3 lbs. per

    A. square inch   B. square foot
    C. square yard   D. sheet

22.____

23. The MAIN reason for using flashing at the intersection of different roof planes is to

    A. increase the durability of the shingles
    B. simplify the installation of the shingles
    C. waterproof the roof
    D. improve the appearance of the roof

23.____

24. Of the following roofing materials, the one that is MOST frequently used in *built-up* roofs is

    A. asbestos shingles   B. three-ply felt
    C. sheet copper   D. wood sheathing

24.____

25. As used in roofing, *a square* refers to

    A. a tool for lining up the roofing with the eaves of the house
    B. one hundred square feet of roofing
    C. one hundred shingles of roofing
    D. one hundred pounds of roofing

25.____

26. In the process of replacing a pane of window glass, the old putty should be scraped off the window sash and the wood surfaces then primed with

    A. resin oil
    B. shellac
    C. linseed oil
    D. enamel

27. The LARGEST available size of glazier's points is number

    A. 3   B. 1   C. 0   D. 000

28. The purpose of priming wood window sash before applying putty and glass is to prevent the

    A. putty from absorbing moisture from the wood
    B. putty from staining the wood
    C. wood from absorbing the oils from the putty
    D. natural wood resins from making the putty brittle

29. When hard, dry putty must be removed from a wood window frame in order to put in a new pane of glass, the BEST tool with which to do this job is a

    A. screwdriver
    B. putty knife
    C. wide wood chisel
    D. pocket knife

30. Before repainting a wood surface on which the old paint film has developed some wrinkling, the MOST appropriate treatment for the wood surface is a

    A. thorough scraping
    B. light shellacking
    C. wash-down with dilute muriatic acid
    D. rubbing down of the wrinkles with fairly coarse sand-paper

31. A paint that is characterized by its ability to dry to an especially smooth, hard, glossy or semi-glossy finish is called a(n)

    A. primer   B. sealer   C. glaze   D. enamel

32. The BEST thinner for varnish is

    A. gasoline
    B. turpentine
    C. kerosene
    D. water

33. To get a good paint job on a new plaster wall, one should make certain that the

    A. wall is thoroughly dry before painting
    B. base coat is much darker than the finishing coat
    C. wall has been roughened enough to make the paint stick
    D. plaster has not completely set

34. In a three-coat plaster job, the brown coat is applied

    A. before the scratch coat has set
    B. immediately after the scratch coat
    C. after the scratch coat has set and partially dried
    D. after the scratch coat has thoroughly dried out

35. Plaster which has sand as an aggregate, when compared with plaster which has a light-weight aggregate, is

    A. a better sound absorber
    B. a better insulator
    C. less likely to crack under a sharp blow
    D. cheaper

36. One form of metal lath comes in sheets 27" x 96".
    The number of sheets required to cover 20 square yards without overlap is

    A. 9   B. 10   C. 11   D. 12

37. When nailing gypsum board lath to studs or furring strips, the nailing should be started_____ of the board.

    A. along the top
    B. along the bottom
    C. at the center
    D. at one end

38. A wooden mortar box for slaking lime is lined with sheet iron.
    Of the following, the GREATEST advantage of the lining is that

    A. a better grade putty is produced
    B. the box is easier to clean
    C. it makes the box water-tight
    D. it prevents burning of the wood

39. The Building Code requires that water used in plastering MUST

    A. be perfectly clear in color
    B. not have any rust in it
    C. be fit for drinking
    D. not be fluoridated

40. In order to prevent thin sheet metal from buckling when riveting it to an angle iron, the BEST procedure is to

    A. start riveting at one end of the sheet and work toward the other end
    B. start riveting at both ends of the sheet and work in toward the center
    C. install alternate rivets working in one direction, and then fill in the remaining rivets working in the other direction
    D. start riveting in the center of the joint, working out in both directions

KEY (CORRECT ANSWERS)

1.	B	11.	B	21.	B	31.	D
2.	C	12.	B	22.	B	32.	B
3.	C	13.	B	23.	C	33.	A
4.	C	14.	D	24.	B	34.	C
5.	A	15.	C	25.	B	35.	D
6.	C	16.	A	26.	C	36.	B
7.	B	17.	D	27.	C	37.	C
8.	C	18.	D	28.	C	38.	B
9.	C	19.	A	29.	C	39.	C
10.	D	20.	A	30.	D	40.	D

TEST 2

DIRECTIONS: Each question or incomplete statement is followed by several suggested answers or completions. Select the one that BEST answers the question or completes the statement. *PRINT THE LETTER OF THE CORRECT ANSWER IN THE SPACE AT THE RIGHT.*

1. A drill bit measures .625 inches.
   The FRACTIONAL EQUIVALENT, in inches, is

   A. 9/16   B. 5/8   C. 11/16   D. 3/4

   1.____

2. The number of cubic yards of sand required to fill a bin measuring 12 feet by 6 feet by 4 feet is MOST NEARLY

   A. 8   B. 11   C. 48   D. 96

   2.____

3. Assume that you are assigned to put down floor tiles in a room measuring 8 feet by 10 feet. Individual tiles measure 9 inches by 9 inches.
   The total number of floor tiles required to cover the entire floor is MOST NEARLY

   A. 107   B. 121   C. 144   D. 160

   3.____

4. Lumber is usually sold by the board foot, and a board foot is defined as a board one foot square and one inch thick.
   If the price of one board foot of lumber is 18 cents and you need 20 feet of lumber 6 inches wide and 1 inch thick, the cost of the 20 feet of the lumber is

   A. $1.80   B. $2.40   C. $3.60   D. $4.80

   4.____

5. For a certain plumbing repair job, you need three lengths of pipe, 12 1/4 inches, 6 1/2 inches, and 8 5/8 inches.
   If you cut these three lengths from the same piece of pipe, which is 36 inches long, and each cut consumes 1/8 inch of pipe, the length of pipe REMAINING after you have cut out your three pieces should be _____ inches.

   A. 7 1/4   B. 7 7/8   C. 8 1/4   D. 8 7/8

   5.____

6. Glazier points are small pieces of galvanized metal often having the shape of a(n)

   A. circle   B. ellipse   C. square   D. triangle

   6.____

7. Putty that is too stiff is made workable by adding

   A. gasoline   B. linseed oil
   C. water   D. lacquer thinner

   7.____

8. Soap is applied to wood screws before they are used in order to

   A. prevent rust
   B. make a tight fit
   C. make insertion easier
   D. prevent screws from loosening after insertion

   8.____

9. A method sometimes used to prevent a pipe from buckling during a bending operation is to

   9.____

35

A. bend the pipe very quickly
B. keep the seam of the pipe on the outside of the bend
C. nick the pipe at the center of the bend
D. pack the inside of the pipe with sand

10. Rubber gaskets are frequently placed between the faces of the flanges when making up a flanged joint in a pipe line in order to

A. prevent corrosion of the machined faces
B. permit full tightening of the flange bolts without danger of thread stripping
C. eliminate the necessity for accurate alignment of the pipe
D. make a tight joint

11. A parapet is the

A. stepping out of successive courses of brickwork
B. continuation of a wall above the roof line
C. wall enclosing stairs that lead to the roof
D. portion of an exterior wall below a window

12. The process of removing the insulation from a wire is called

A. braiding   B. skinning   C. sweating   D. tinning

13. The process of making fresh concrete watertight, durable, and strong after it has been poured is called

A. air-entraining
B. finishing
C. curing
D. accelerating

14. A mixture of cement, sand, and water is called

A. hydrated lime
B. plain concrete
C. hydrated cement
D. mortar

15. The *grip* applied to a pipe with gas pliers is increased by using pliers with

A. longer handles
B. larger jaws
C. thicker handles
D. larger teeth

16. Those materials which are added to a paint vehicle to regulate its consistency and thus increase its spreading power and facilitate its application are called

A. driers
B. thinners
C. extenders
D. oxidents

17. The fitting which usually is easiest to disconnect FIRST when disassembling a piping run is a(n)

A. cross
B. union
C. return bend
D. elbow

18. For convenience in case of future repairs to a long pipe line, it is DESIRABLE to fit the pipe together with several

A. street ells
B. elbows
C. return bends
D. unions

19. If four pipes are to be connected into each other at a common point, it would be NECESSARY to use a(n)

    A. tee fitting
    B. street ell
    C. cross
    D. offset

20. The BEST of the following tools to use for cutting off a piece of single conductor #6 rubber insulated lead covered cable is a

    A. pair of electrician's pliers
    B. hacksaw
    C. hammer and cold chisel
    D. lead knife

21. One ADVANTAGE of rubber insulation is that it

    A. does not deteriorate with age
    B. is able to withstand high temperature
    C. does not absorb much moisture
    D. is not damaged by oil

22. The SIMPLEST device for interrupting an overloaded electrical circuit is a

    A. fuse
    B. relay
    C. capacitor
    D. choke-coil

23. Reinforced concrete USUALLY means concrete that has been strengthened by use of

    A. additional cement
    B. steel bars
    C. extra heavy gravel
    D. high strength cement

24. A VERTICAL wood member in the wall of a wood frame house is known as a

    A. stringer
    B. ridge member
    C. stud
    D. header

25. A riser is GENERALLY a pipe run which is

    A. horizontal
    B. curved
    C. vertical
    D. at a 45-degree angle

26. A standard pipe thread DIFFERS from a standard screw thread in that the pipe thread

    A. is tapered
    B. is deeper
    C. requires no lubrication when cutting
    D. has the same pitch for any diameter of pipe

27. The material which is LEAST likely to be found in use as the outer covering of rubber insulated wires or cables is

    A. cotton
    B. varnished cambric
    C. lead
    D. neoprene

28. In measuring to determine the size of a standard insulated conductor, the PROPER place to use the wire gauge is on

A. the insulation
B. the outer covering
C. the stranded conductor
D. one strand of the conductor

29. Rubber insulation on an electrical conductor would MOST quickly be damaged by continuous contact with   29.____

    A. acid   B. water   C. oil   D. alkali

30. If a fuse clip becomes hot under normal circuit load, the MOST probable cause is that the   30.____

    A. clip makes poor contact with the fuse ferrule
    B. circuit wires are too small
    C. current rating of the fuse is too high
    D. voltage rating of the fuse is too low

31. If the input to a 10 to 1 step-down transformer is 15 amperes at 2400 volts, the secondary output would be NEAREST to _____ amperes at _____ volts.   31.____

    A. 1.5; 24,000   B. 150; 240
    C. 1.5; 240   D. 150; 24,000

32. The resistance of a copper wire to the flow of electricity _____ as the _____ of the wire _____.   32.____

    A. increases; diameter; increases
    B. decreases; diameter; decreases
    C. decreases; length; increases
    D. increases; length; increases

33. Where galvanized steel conduit is used, the PRIMARY purpose of the galvanizing is to   33.____

    A. increase mechanical strength
    B. retard rusting
    C. provide a good surface for painting
    D. provide good electrical contact for grounding

34. The lamps used for station and tunnel lighting in the subways are generally operated at slightly less than their rated voltage.
    The LOGICAL reason for this is to   34.____

    A. prevent overloading of circuits
    B. increase the life of the lamps
    C. decrease glare
    D. obtain a more even distribution of light

35. The CORRECT method of measuring the power taken by an a.c. electric motor is to use a   35.____

    A. wattmeter
    B. voltmeter and an ammeter
    C. power factor meter
    D. tachometer

36. Wood ladders should NOT be painted because the paint   36.____

    A. may deteriorate the wood
    B. makes the ladders slippery
    C. is inflammable
    D. may cover cracks or defects

37. Goggles would be LEAST necessary when   37.____

    A. recharging soda-acid fire extinguishers
    B. chipping stone
    C. putting electrolyte into an Edison battery
    D. scraping rubber insulation from a wire

38. The number and type of precautions to be taken on a job generally depend LEAST on the   38.____

    A. nature of the job
    B. length of time the job is expected to last
    C. kind of tools and materials being used
    D. location of the work

39. When training workers in the use of tools and equipment, safety precautions related to their use should be FIRST mentioned   39.____

    A. in the introductory training session before the workers begin to use the equipment or tools
    B. during training sessions when workers practice operating the tools or equipment
    C. after the workers are qualified to use the equipment in their daily tasks
    D. when an agency safety bulletin related to the tools and equipment is received

40. Many portable electric power tools, such as electric drills, have a third conductor in the power lead which is used to connect the case of the tool to a grounded part of the electric outlet.   40.____
    The reason for this extra conductor is to

    A. have a spare wire in case one power wire should break
    B. strengthen the power lead so it cannot easily be damaged
    C. prevent the user of the tool from being shocked
    D. enable the tool to be used for long periods of time without overheating

KEY (CORRECT ANSWERS)

1.	B	11.	B	21.	C	31.	B
2.	B	12.	B	22.	A	32.	D
3.	C	13.	C	23.	B	33.	B
4.	A	14.	D	24.	C	34.	B
5.	C	15.	A	25.	C	35.	A
6.	D	16.	B	26.	A	36.	D
7.	B	17.	B	27.	B	37.	D
8.	C	18.	D	28.	D	38.	B
9.	D	19.	C	29.	C	39.	A
10.	D	20.	B	30.	A	40.	C

EXAMINATION SECTION
TEST 1

DIRECTIONS: Each question or incomplete statement is followed by several suggested answers or completions. Select the one that BEST answers the question or completes the statement. *PRINT THE LETTER OF THE CORRECT ANSWER IN THE SPACE AT THE RIGHT.*

1. The combustion efficiency of a boiler can be determined with a CO_2 indicator and the   1.____

    A. under fire draft
    B. boiler room humidity
    C. flue gas temperature
    D. outside air temperature

2. A quick, practical method of determining if the cast-iron waste pipe delivered to a job has been damaged in transit is to   2.____

    A. hydraulically test it
    B. "ring" each length with a hammer
    C. drop each length to see whether it breaks
    D. visually examine the pipe for cracks

3. An electrostatic precipitator is used to   3.____

    A. filter the air supply
    B. remove sludge from the fuel oil
    C. remove particles from the fuel gas
    D. supply samples for an Orsat analysis

4. The PRIMARY cause of cracking and spalling of refractory lining in the furnace of a steam generator is *most likely* due to   4.____

    A. continuous over-firing of boiler
    B. slag accumulation on furnace walls
    C. change in fuel from solid to liquid
    D. uneven heating and cooling within the refractory brick

5. The term "effective temperature" in air conditioning means   5.____

    A. the dry bulb temperature
    B. the average of the wet and dry bulb temperatures
    C. the square root of the product of wet and dry bulb temperatures
    D. an arbitrary index combining the effects of temperature, humidity, and movement

6. The piping in all buildings having dual water distribution systems should be identified by a color coding of _____ for potable water lines and _____ for non-potable water lines.   6.____

    A. green; red
    B. green; yellow
    C. yellow; green
    D. yellow; red

7. The breaking of a component of a machine subjected to excessive vibration is called   7.____

    A. tensile failure
    B. fatigue failure
    C. caustic embrittlement
    D. amplitude failure

8. The TWO MOST important factors to be considered in selecting fans for ventilating systems are

    A. noise and efficiency
    B. space available and weight
    C. first cost and dimensional bulk
    D. construction and arrangement of drive

9. In the modern power plant deaerator, air is removed from water to

    A. reduce heat losses in the heaters
    B. reduce corrosion of boiler steel due to the air
    C. reduce the load of the main condenser air pumps
    D. prevent pumps from becoming vapor bound

10. The abbreviations BOD, COD, and DO are associated with

    A. flue gas analysis
    B. air pollution control
    C. boiler water treatment
    D. water pollution control

11. The piping of a newly installed drainage system should be tested upon completion of the rough plumbing with a head of water of NOT LESS THAN _____ feet.

    A. 10   B. 15   C. 20   D. 25

12. Of the following statements concerning aquastats, the one which is CORRECT is:

    A. Aquastats may be obtained with either a narrow or wide range of settings
    B. Aquastats have a mercury tube switch which is controlled by the stack switch
    C. An aquastat is a device used to shut down the burner in the event of low water in the boiler
    D. An aquastat should be located about 4 inches above the normal water line of the boiler

13. The SAFEST way to protect the domestic water supply from contamination by sewage or non-potable water is to insert

    A. air gaps
    B. swing connections
    C. double check valves
    D. tanks with overhead discharge

14. The MAIN function of a back-pressure valve which is sometimes found in the connection between a water drain pipe and the sewer system is to

    A. equalize the pressure between the drain pipe and the sewer
    B. prevent sewer water from flowing into the drain pipe
    C. provide pressure to enable waste to reach the sewer
    D. make sure that there is not too much water pressure in the sewer line

15. Boiler water is neutral if its pH value is

    A. 0   B. 1   C. 7   D. 14

16. A domestic hot water mixing or tempering valve should be preceded in the hot water line by a

    A. strainer
    B. foot valve
    C. check valve
    D. steam trap

17. Between a steam boiler and its safety valve there should be

    A. no valve of any type
    B. a gate valve of the same size as the safety valve
    C. a swing check valve of at least the same size as the safety valve
    D. a cock having a clear opening equal in area to the pipe connecting the boiler and safety valve

18. A diagram of horizontal plumbing drainage lines should have cleanouts shown

    A. at least every 25 feet
    B. at least every 100 feet
    C. wherever a basin is located
    D. wherever a change in direction occurs

19. When a Bourdon gauge is used to measure steam pressures, some form of siphon or water seal must be maintained.
    The reason for this is to

    A. obtain "absolute" pressure readings
    B. prevent steam from entering the gage
    C. prevent condensate from entering the gage
    D. obtain readings below atmospheric pressure

20. In a closed heat exchanger, oil is cooled by condensate which is to be returned to a boiler. In order to avoid the possibility of contaminating the condensate with oil should a tube fail in the oil cooler, it would be good practice to

    A. cool the oil by air instead of water
    B. treat the condensate with an oil solvent
    C. keep the oil pressure in the exchanger higher than the water pressure
    D. keep the water pressure in the exchanger higher than the oil pressure

21. A radiator thermostatic trap is used on a vacuum return type of heating system to

    A. release the pocketed air only
    B. reduce the amount of condensate
    C. maintain a predetermined radiator water level
    D. prevent the return of live steam to the return line

22. According to the color coding of piping, fire protection piping should be painted

    A. green   B. yellow   C. purple   D. red

23. The MAIN purpose of a standpipe system is to

    A. supply the roof water tank
    B. provide water for firefighting

C. circulate water for the heating system
D. provide adequate pressure for the water supply

24. The name "Saybolt" is associated with the measurement of 24.___

   A. viscosity
   B. Btu content
   C. octane rating
   D. temperature

25. Recirculation of conditioned air in an air-conditioned building is done MAINLY to 25.___

   A. reduce refrigeration tonnage required
   B. increase room entrophy
   C. increase air specific humidity
   D. reduce room temperature below the dewpoint

26. In a plumbing installation, vent pipes are GENERALLY used to 26.___

   A. prevent the loss of water seal from traps by evaporation
   B. prevent the loss of water seal due to several causes other than evaporation
   C. act as an additional path for liquids to flow through during normal use of a plumbing fixture
   D. prevent the backflow of water in a cross-connection between a drinking water line and a sewage line

27. The designation "150 W" cast on the bonnet of a gate valve is an indication of the 27.___

   A. water working temperature
   B. water working pressure
   C. area of the opening in square inches
   D. weight of the valve in pounds

28. In the city, the size soil pipe necessary in a sewage drainage system is determined by the 28.___

   A. legal occupancy of the building
   B. vertical height of the soil line
   C. number of restrooms connected to the soil line
   D. number of "fixture units" connected to the soil line

29. Fins or other extended surfaces are used on heat exchanger tubes when 29.___

   A. the exchanger is a water-to-water exchanger
   B. water is on one side of the tube and condensing steam on the other side
   C. the surface coefficient of heat transfer on both sides of the tube is high
   D. the surface coefficient of heat transfer on one side of the tube is low compared to the coefficient on the other side of the tube

30. A fusible plug may be put in a fire tube boiler as an emergency device to indicate low water level. The fusible plug is installed so that under normal operating conditions, 30.___

   A. both sides are exposed to steam
   B. one side is exposed to water and the other side to steam
   C. one side is exposed to steam and the other side to hot gases
   D. one side is exposed to the water and the other side to hot gases

31. Extra strong wrought-iron pipe, as compared to standard wrought-iron pipe of the same nominal size, has

    A. the same outside diameter but a smaller inside diameter
    B. the same inside diameter but a larger outside diameter
    C. a larger outside diameter and a smaller inside diameter
    D. larger inside and outside diameters

32. Fans may be rated on a dynamic or a static efficiency basis. The dynamic efficiency would *probably* be

    A. lower in value because of the energy absorbed by the air velocity
    B. the same as the static in the case of centrifugal blowers running at various speeds
    C. the same as the static in the case of axial flow blowers running at various speeds
    D. higher in value than the static

33. The function of the stack relay in an oil burner installation is to

    A. regulate the draft over the fire
    B. regulate the flow of fuel oil to the burner
    C. stop the motor if the oil has not ignited
    D. stop the motor if the water or steam pressure is too high

34. The type of centrifugal pump which is inherently balanced for hydraulic thrust is the

    A. double suction impeller type
    B. single suction impeller type
    C. single stage type
    D. multistage type

35. The specifications for a job using sheet lead calls for "4-lb. sheet lead." This means that each sheet should weigh

    A. 4 lbs.
    B. 4 lbs. per square
    C. 4 lbs. per square foot
    D. 4 lbs. per cubic inch

36. The total cooling load design conditions for a building are divided for convenience into two components.
    These are:

    A. infiltration and radiation
    B. sensible heat and latent heat
    C. wet and dry bulb temperatures
    D. solar heat gain and moisture transfer

37. The function of a Hartford loop used on some steam boilers is to

    A. limit boiler steam pressure
    B. limit temperature of the steam
    C. prevent high water levels in the boiler
    D. prevent back flow of water from the boiler into the return main

38. Vibration from a ventilating blower can be prevented from being transmitted to the duct work by

   A. installing straighteners in the duct
   B. throttling the air supply to the blower
   C. bolting the blower tightly to the duct
   D. installing a canvas sleeve at the blower outlet

39. A specification states that access panels to suspended ceiling will be of metal. The MAIN reason for providing access panels is to

   A. improve the insulation of the ceiling
   B. improve the appearance of the ceiling
   C. make it easier to construct the building
   D. make it easier to maintain the building

40. A plumber on a job reports that the steamfitter has installed a 3" steam line in a location at which the plans show the house trap. On inspecting the job, you should

   A. tell the steamfitter to remove the steam line
   B. study the condition to see if the house trap can be relocated
   C. tell the plumber and steamfitter to work it out between themselves and then report to you
   D. tell the plumber to find another location for the trap because the steamfitter has already completed his work

41. In the installation of any heating system, the MOST important consideration is that

   A. all elements be made of a good grade of cast iron
   B. all radiators and connectors be mounted horizontally
   C. the smallest velocity of flow of heating medium be used
   D. there be proper clearance between hot surfaces and surrounding combustible material

42. Which one of the following is the PRIMARY object in drawing up a set of specifications for materials to be purchased?

   A. Control of quality
   B. Outline of intended use
   C. Establishment of standard sizes
   D. Location and method of inspection.

43. The drawing which should be used as a LEGAL reference when checking completed construction work is the _____ drawing.

   A. contract
   B. assembly
   C. working or shop
   D. preliminary

Questions 44-50.

DIRECTIONS: Questions 44 through 50 refer to the plumbing drawing shown below.

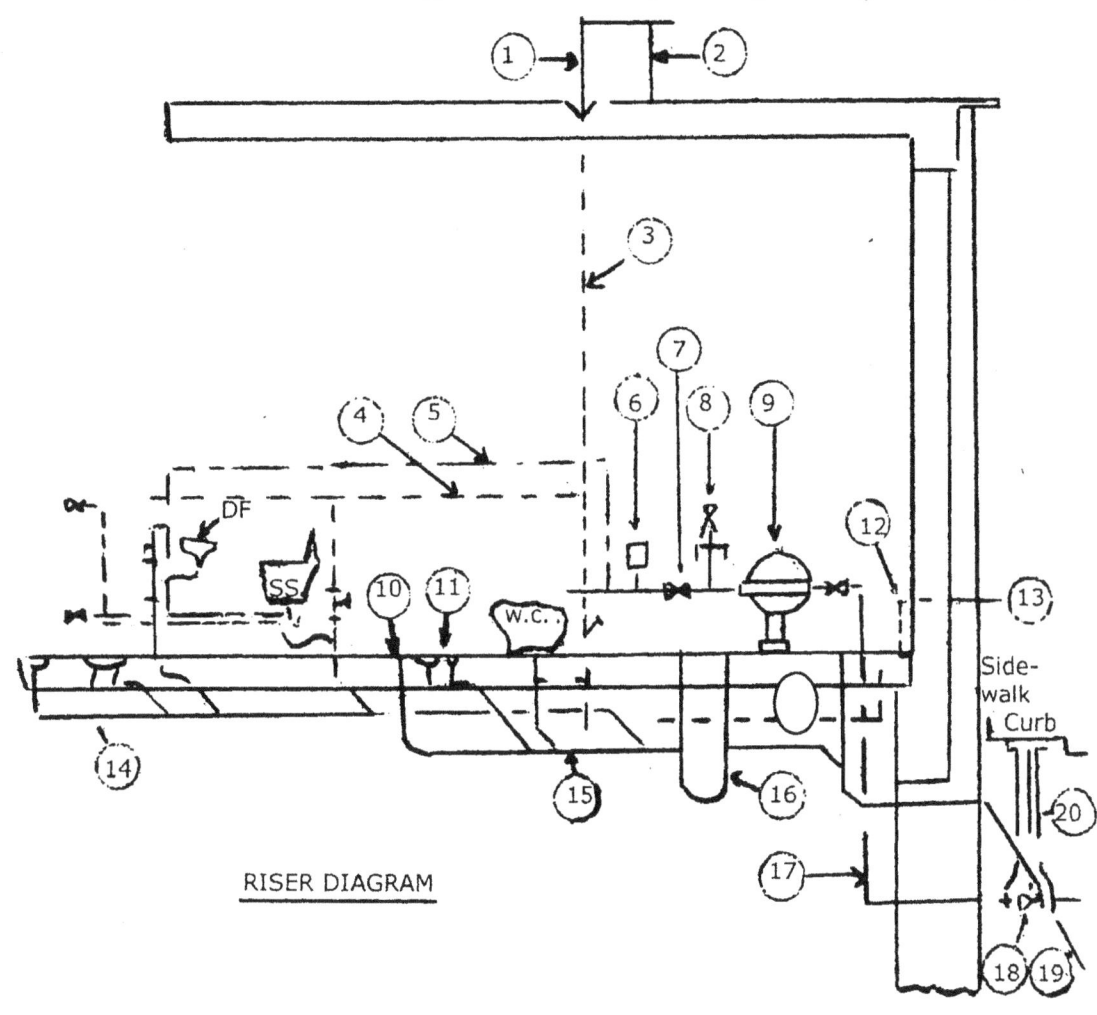

RISER DIAGRAM

44. According to the building code, the MINIMUM diameter of No. 1 and its minimum height, No. 2 respectively, are

    A. 2" and 12"
    B. 3" and 18"
    C. 4" and 24"
    D. 6" and 36"

44.____

45. No. 6 is a

    A. relief valve
    B. shock absorber
    C. testing connection
    D. drain

45.____

46. No. 9 is a

    A. strainer
    B. float valve
    C. meter
    D. pedestal

46.____

47. No. 11 is a

    A. floor drain
    B. cleanout
    C. trap
    D. vent connection

47.____

8 (#1)

48. No. ⟨13⟩ is a

    A. standpipe
    B. air inlet
    C. sprinkler head
    D. cleanout

49. The size of No. ⟨16⟩ is

    A. 2" x 2"
    B. 2" x 3"
    C. 3" x 3"
    D. 4" x 4"

50. No. ⟨18⟩ is a

    A. pressure reducing valve
    B. butterfly valve
    C. curb cock
    D. sprinkler head

KEY (CORRECT ANSWERS)

1. C	11. A	21. D	31. A	41. D
2. B	12. C	22. D	32. D	42. A
3. C	13. A	23. B	33. C	43. A
4. D	14. B	24. A	34. A	44. C
5. D	15. C	25. A	35. C	45. B
6. B	16. A	26. B	36. B	46. C
7. B	17. A	27. B	37. D	47. A
8. A	18. D	28. D	38. D	48. B
9. B	19. B	29. D	39. D	49. D
10. D	20. D	30. D	40. B	50. C

EXAMINATION SECTION
TEST 1

DIRECTIONS: Each question or incomplete statement is followed by several suggested answers or completions. Select the one that BEST answers the question or completes the statement. *PRINT THE LETTER OF THE CORRECT ANSWER IN THE SPACE AT THE RIGHT.*

Questions 1-5.

DIRECTIONS: For Questions 1 through 5, inclusive, Column I lists frequently used construction terms. Column II lists some of the building trades. For each item listed in Column I, enter in the appropriate space at the right the capital letter in front of the trade listed in Column II that is MOST closely associated with the item. Each trade may be used more than once or not at all.

COLUMN I	COLUMN II
1. Bed	A. Plumbing
2. Wiping	B. Plastering
3. Brown	C. Carpentry
4. Key	D. Masonry
5. Bridging	E. Painting
	F. Steelwork
	G. Roofing

6. A *cricket* would be found

    A. on a roof
    B. at a structural steel connection
    C. supporting reinforcing steel
    D. over a window

7. *Cutting in* is done when

    A. trimming a stud to size
    B. fitting a bat in a brick wall
    C. painting in tight corners
    D. trimming tallow for a wiped joint

8. *Corbeling* results in

    A. strengthening a concrete column
    B. waterproofing a foundation wall
    C. anchoring a steel girder to a bearing wall
    D. increasing the thickness of a brick wall

9. Solder used for copper gutters is MOST frequently

   A. 30-70   B. 40-60   C. 50-50   D. 60-40

10. A jack rafter runs from

    A. plate to ridge
    B. hip to ridge
    C. plate to hip
    D. plate to plate

11. The one of the following items that is LEAST related to the others is

    A. sill   B. joist   C. sole   D. newel

12. A *fire cut* is made on

    A. timber posts
    B. rafters
    C. floor joists
    D. lathing

13. The one of the following items that is LEAST related to the others is

    A. joist hanger
    B. pintle
    C. bridle iron
    D. stirrup

14. The PROPER order of nailing sub-flooring and bridging is

    A. top of bridging, bottom of bridging, sub-flooring
    B. bottom of bridging, sub-flooring, top of bridging
    C. top of bridging, sub-flooring, bottom of bridging
    D. bottom of bridging, top of bridging, sub-flooring

15. Sleepers would be found in

    A. walls   B. doors   C. footings   D. floors

16. The one of the following woods that is MOST commonly used for finish flooring is

    A. hemlock   B. cypress   C. larch   D. oak

17. Spacing of studs in a stud partition is MOST frequently _____" o.c.

    A. 12   B. 14   C. 16   D. 18

18. A hollow masonry wall should be used in preference to a solid masonry wall when the characteristic MOST desired is

    A. insulation
    B. strength
    C. beauty
    D. durability

19. The arrangement of headers and stretchers in brickwork is known as the

    A. bond   B. stringer   C. lacing   D. stile

20. Of the following, the reason that is LEAST likely to justify pointing brickwork is that pointing _____ the wall.

    A. improves the appearance of
    B. helps prevent cracking of
    C. increases the useful life of
    D. helps waterproof

21. The purpose of flashing is to

    A. keep water out
    B. speed the set of mortar
    C. anchor a cornice
    D. cover exposed joists

22. The one of the following classes of wall that would LEAST likely be the outside wall of a building is a

    A. spandrel   B. fire   C. curtain   D. parapet

23. Lime is added to mortar USUALLY to

    A. increase the strength of the mortar
    B. make the mortar water resistant
    C. make it easier to apply the mortar
    D. improve the appearance of the mortar joint

24. Efflorescence on the face of a brick wall is BEST removed by scrubbing with a solution of

    A. muriatic acid
    B. sodium silicate
    C. oxalic acid
    D. calcium oxide

25. The one of the following that is NOT a defect in painting is

    A. chalking
    B. checking
    C. alligatoring
    D. waning

26. The one of the following ingredients of a paint that would be called the *vehicle* is

    A. white lead
    B. turpentine
    C. linseed oil
    D. pigment

27. The one of the following that is used as a rust preventative in the prime coat for painting steel is

    A. aluminum
    B. red lead
    C. titanium dioxide
    D. carbon black

28. *Boxing*, with reference to paint, means

    A. thinning   B. mixing   C. spreading   D. drying

29. When painting new wood, filling of nail holes and cracks with putty should be done

    A. 24 hours before priming
    B. immediately before priming
    C. after priming and before the second coat
    D. after the second coat and before the finish coat

30. The one of the following that is the size of a reinforcing rod MOST commonly used in reinforced concrete construction is

    A. 1 3/4" ϕ B. 18 gauge   C. #9   D. 2 ST3

31. Honeycombing in concrete is USUALLY caused by

    A. too plastic a mix
    B. high fall of concrete
    C. mixing too long
    D. inadequate vibration

32. A concrete mix is indicated as 1:2:3 1/2 mix. The number 2 refers to the proportion by volume of

    A. water   B. cement   C. gravel   D. sand

33. Specifications for concrete mixes frequently call for the use of dry sand. The reason for this is that the additional water in wet sand will

    A. make it more difficult to place the concrete
    B. decrease the strength of the concrete
    C. cause the sand and stone to segregate
    D. increase the cost of waterproofing

34. Curing of concrete serves PRIMARILY to

    A. prevent freezing of the concrete
    B. permit early removal of forms
    C. delay setting of the concrete
    D. prevent evaporation of moisture

35. The MAIN reason that forms for concrete work are oiled is to

    A. *permit* easy removal of forms
    B. *prevent* rust marks on the concrete
    C. *prevent* bleeding of water
    D. *permit* easier vibration of the concrete

36. The one of the following terms that is LEAST related to the others is

    A. 5-ply   B. mastic
    C. vapor barrier D. flashing

37. Before quicklime can be used for plaster, it must be

    A. slaked   B. burned   C. floated   D. glazed

38. When a hard plaster is required, as in halls, the one of the following that would MOST likely be used is

    A. lime   B. Keene's cement
    C. stucco   D. marbling

39. To give plaster a hard finish, hydrated lime is mixed with

    A. white cement   B. linseed oil putty
    C. white lead   D. plaster of paris

40. The purpose of a ground in plaster work is to

    A. provide a key for the plaster
    B. help the plasterer make an even wall
    C. prevent the plasterer's scaffold from slipping
    D. hold the loose plaster before it is placed

41. When a lightweight plaster is required, the one of the following fine aggregates that is MOST likely to be used is

    A. cinders
    B. sand
    C. talc
    D. vermiculite

42. Of the following fireproofing materials, the one which would be MOST frequently used to fireproof steel columns in a fireproof building is

    A. sheet rock
    B. vermiculite plaster
    C. brick
    D. rock lath

43. The one of the following items that is LEAST related to the others is

    A. rock wool
    B. wall board
    C. sheet rock
    D. rock lath

44. The first layer of plaster placed in a 3-coat plaster job is called the _____ coat.

    A. brown   B. scratch   C. hard   D. white

45. The one of the following symbols that represents a steel section which is MOST similar in appearance to a W section is

    A. U   B. L   C. I   D. Z

46. A plate used to connect two steel angles in a roof truss is known as a(n)

    A. angle iron
    B. gusset plate
    C. bearing plate
    D. tie bar

47. Steel beams are COMMONLY anchored to brick walls by

    A. government anchors
    B. tie rods
    C. eye bars
    D. anchor bolts

48. Rivet holes are lined up with a

    A. set screw
    B. ginnywink
    C. drift pin
    D. trivet

49. A sewer that carries BOTH storm water and sewage is called a _____ sewer.

    A. sanitary   B. flush   C. combined   D. mixed

50. A fresh air inlet for a house drainage system would be connected to the system

    A. just ahead of the house trap
    B. at each horizontal branch line
    C. at the top of the stack through the roof
    D. at the trap of each water closet

KEY (CORRECT ANSWERS)

1. D	11. D	21. A	31. D	41. D
2. A	12. C	22. B	32. D	42. B
3. B	13. B	23. C	33. B	43. A
4. B	14. C	24. A	34. D	44. B
5. C	15. D	25. D	35. A	45. C
6. A	16. D	26. C	36. C	46. B
7. C	17. C	27. B	37. A	47. A
8. D	18. A	28. B	38. B	48. C
9. C	19. A	29. C	39. D	49. C
10. C	20. B	30. C	40. B	50. A

TEST 2

DIRECTIONS: Each question or incomplete statement is followed by several suggested answers or completions. Select the one that BEST answers the question or completes the statement. *PRINT THE LETTER OF THE CORRECT ANSWER IN THE SPACE AT THE RIGHT.*

Questions 1-5.

DIRECTIONS: Column I consists of a list of trades, and Column II lists tools used in those trades. In the space at the right, opposite the number of the trade in Column I, write the letter preceding the tool of the trade in Column II.

	COLUMN I		COLUMN II	
1.	Carpenter	A.	Mop	1.____
2.	Plumber	B.	Hawk	2.____
3.	Plasterer	C.	Miter box	3.____
4.	Bricklayer	D.	Shave-hook	4.____
5.	Roofer	E.	Jointing tool	5.____

Questions 6-7.

DIRECTIONS: Questions 6 and 7 refer to the mortar joints shown below.

6. The mortar joint MOST frequently used on common brickwork is   6.____
   A. 1   B. 2   C. 3   D. 4

7. The mortar joint which would NOT usually be made unless an outside scaffold was used is   7.____
   A. 1   B. 2   C. 3   D. 4

8. A rectangular yard is 50'0" long by 8'6" wide.   8.____
   The area of the yard is, in square feet,
   A. 420.0   B. 422.5   C. 425.0   D. 427.5

9. A rectangular court is 23'0" long by 9'6" wide. 9.____
   The length of the diagonal is MOST NEARLY

   A. 24'8"   B. 24'10"   C. 25'2"   D. 25'6"

10. Concrete weighs 150 pounds per cubic foot. 10.____
    A slab of concrete 6'0" long by 3'6" wide by 1'4" thick weighs MOST NEARLY _____ pounds.

    A. 4150   B. 4200   C. 4250   D. 4300

11. A building 32'0" by 65'0" occupies a lot 60'0" by 110'0". The ratio of building area to lot 11.____
    area is MOST NEARLY

    A. 0.32   B. 0.33   C. 0.34   D. 0.35

12. When painting wood, puttying of nail holes and cracks is done 12.____

    A. before any painting is started
    B. after the priming coat is applied
    C. after the finish coat is applied
    D. at any stage in the painting

13. The process of pouring paint from one container to another in order to mix it is known as 13.____

    A. bleeding   B. boxing   C. cutting   D. stirring

14. Paint is *thinned* with 14.____

    A. linseed oil   B. turpentine
    C. varnish   D. gasoline

15. A wood screw which can be tightened by a wrench is known as a _____ screw. 15.____

    A. lag   B. Philips   C. carriage   D. monkey

16. To permit easy removal of forms from concrete, the inside surfaces of the forms are often 16.____
    coated with

    A. paint   B. oil   C. water   D. asphalt

17. Sixteen pieces of 2 x 4 lumber, each 10'6" long, contain a total of _____ FBM. 17.____

    A. 110   B. 111   C. 112   D. 113

18. The consistency of concrete is measured with a 18.____

    A. Vicat needle   B. slump cone
    C. hook gage   D. bourdon gage

19. End-matched lumber would MOST likely be used for 19.____

    A. sheathing   B. roofing   C. flooring   D. siding

20. A post or shore is to be placed midway between columns to support the formwork for a 20.____
    reinforced concrete girder. The post should be cut

    A. short, so that wedging is required
    B. to exact length

C. long, so that it will have to be driven into place
D. in two pieces, to permit jackknifing into place

21. Batter boards are set by a 21.____

    A. mason   B. plumber   C. roofer   D. surveyor

22. Of the following terms, all of which refer to tools, the one which is LEAST related to the others is 22.____

    A. back   B. box-end   C. cross-cut   D. rip

23. Of the following tools, the one which is LEAST like the others is 23.____

    A. brace and bit   B. draw-knife
    C. plans   D. spoke-shave

24. When wood splits easily, it is advisable to drill a hole for each nail. The hole for the nail should be _____ the nail. 24.____

    A. larger in diameter than
    B. smaller in diameter than
    C. exactly the same diameter as
    D. less than one-quarter the length of

25. The length of a 10-penny nail, in inches, is 25.____

    A. $2\frac{1}{2}$ B. 3   C. $3\frac{1}{2}$ D. 4

26. The decimal equivalent of 31/64 of an inch is MOST NEARLY 26.____

    A. 0.45   B. 0.46   C. 0.47   D. 0.48

27. Of the following, the one which is BEST classified as an abrasive is 27.____

    A. a saw   B. a chisel   C. graphite   D. sandpaper

28. Of the following construction materials, the one which would MOST likely be stored directly on the ground is 28.____

    A. brick   B. cement   C. steel   D. wood

29. The strength of brick walls is based upon the type of mortar used. The relative strength of the various types of mortar, in descending order, is 29.____

    A. cement, lime, cement-lime
    B. lime, cement-lime, cement
    C. cement-lime, cement, lime
    D. cement, cement-lime, lime

30. Coating reinforcing rods with oil before placing them in the forms is 30.____

    A. *good* practice, because it prevents rusting
    B. *poor* practice, because it makes the rods difficult to handle
    C. *good* practice if the forms are oiled
    D. *poor* practice, because it destroys the bond between the concrete and the rods

31. If the mixing plant should break down after one-half the concrete has been mixed for a floor, the BEST thing to do would be to

   A. take the concrete out of the forms and throw it away
   B. spread the available concrete evenly over the floor area
   C. block off one-half of the floor area and place the available concrete in the blocked-off area
   D. keep mixing the concrete in the forms with shovels until the plant is repaired

32. Splicing of reinforcing bars is accomplished by

   A. using wire ties
   B. underlapping the bars
   C. hooking the bars
   D. using metal clips

33. A sanitary sewer carries

   A. storm water only
   B. sewage only
   C. sewage and storm water
   D. the discharge from a sewage plant

34. A neat line

   A. is the result of good workmanship
   B. is used in concrete construction only
   C. defines an outer limit of a structure
   D. defines an outer limit of excavation for a structure

35. Continued trowelling of a cement-finish floor for a building is

   A. *good* practice, because it provides a smooth floor
   B. *poor* practice, because it produces a slippery floor
   C. *poor* practice, because it brings the fines to the surface
   D. *good* practice, because it insures proper mixing of the cement finish

36. In reinforced concrete form work, a beveled chamfer strip is used to

   A. reinforce the outside of the forms
   B. reinforce the inside of the forms
   C. seal leaks in the forms
   D. do none of the foregoing

37. Cracks in lumber due to contraction along annual rings are known as

   A. checks
   B. wanes
   C. pitch pockets
   D. dry rot

38. Honeycombing is MOST likely to occur in construction involving

   A. steel   B. concrete   C. wood   D. masonry

39. Floor beams are sometimes crowned to

   A. provide arch action
   B. eliminate deflection
   C. strengthen the floor
   D. provide a more nearly level floor than would be provided by straight beams

40. In brickwork, a rowlock course consists of 40.____

    A. headers
    B. stretchers
    C. bricks laid on edge
    D. bricks laid so that the longest dimension is vertical

41. The term *bond,* as used in bricklaying, refers to 41.____

    A. structure only
    B. pattern only
    C. structure and pattern
    D. color and finish of individual bricks

42. Concrete is a mixture of cement, 42.____

    A. fine aggregate, coarse aggregate, and water
    B. sand, and water
    C. stone, and water
    D. sand, and stone

43. Consistency, when used in connection with concrete, refers to the 43.____

    A. seven-day strength
    B. twenty-eight day strength
    C. initial set before forms are removed
    D. plasticity of freshly mixed concrete

44. Brick may be used for the facing material in both faced walls and veneered walls. The distinction between the two types of walls relates to 44.____

    A. bonding or lack of bonding between facing and backing
    B. type of material in facing and backing
    C. relative thickness of facing and backing
    D. the type of mortar used

45. A plaster *key* is NOT formed on _____ lath. 45.____

    A. wood   B. metal
    C. expanded metal D. gypsum

46. Of the following, the BEST tool to use to make a hole in a coping stone is a 46.____

    A. star drill   B. coping saw
    C. pneumatic grinder   D. diamond wheel dresser

47. Roughing refers to work performed by a 47.____

    A. carpenter   B. bricklayer
    C. plumber   D. roofer

48. A post supporting a handrail is known as a 48.____

    A. tread   B. riser   C. newel   D. bevel

49. The live load on a floor is 40 pounds per square foot. The floor joists are on a 14'0" span and are spaced 2'6" on centers.
   The maximum live load carried by a joist, in pounds, is MOST NEARLY

   A. 700 B. 933 C. 1167 D. 1400

50. Of the following terms, the one LEAST related to the others is

   A. ground
   C. rafter
   B. purlin
   D. ridge board

KEY (CORRECT ANSWERS)

1. C	11. A	21. D	31. C	41. C
2. D	12. B	22. B	32. A	42. A
3. B	13. B	23. A	33. B	43. D
4. E	14. B	24. B	34. C	44. A
5. A	15. A	25. B	35. C	45. D
6. C	16. B	26. D	36. D	46. A
7. A	17. C	27. D	37. A	47. C
8. C	18. B	28. A	38. B	48. C
9. B	19. C	29. D	39. D	49. D
10. B	20. A	30. D	40. C	50. A

EXAMINATION SECTION
TEST 1

DIRECTIONS: Each question or incomplete statement is followed by several suggested answers or completions. Select the one that BEST answers the question or completes the statement. *PRINT THE LETTER OF THE CORRECT ANSWER IN THE SPACE AT THE RIGHT.*

Questions 1-3.

DIRECTIONS: Questions 1 through 3, inclusive, are to be answered in accordance with the American Standard Graphical Symbols for Pipe Fittings, Valves, and Piping and American Standard Graphical Symbols for Heating, Ventilating and Air Conditioning.

1. The symbol ⊙─┼─ shown on a piping drawing represents a _____ elbow.

    A. turned down
    B. reducing
    C. long radius
    D. turned up

2. The symbol ──[═]── shown on a heating drawing represents a(n)

    A. expansion joint
    B. hanger or support
    C. heat exchanger
    D. air eliminator

3. The symbol ─┼⋈┼─ shown on a piping drawing represents a _____ gate valve.

    A. welded
    B. flanged
    C. screwed
    D. bell and spigot

4. The MAIN purpose for the inspection of plant equipment, buildings, and facilities is to

    A. determine the quality of maintenance work of all the trades
    B. prevent the overstocking of equipment and materials used in maintenance work
    C. forecast normal maintenance jobs for existing equipment, buildings, and facilities
    D. prevent unscheduled interruptions of operating equipment and excessive deterioration of buildings and facilities

5. Of the following devices, the one that is used to determine the rating, in cubic feet per minute, of a unit ventilator is a(n)

    A. psychrometer
    B. pyrometer
    C. anemometer
    D. manometer

6. A number of 4' x 6' skids loaded with material are to be stored. Assume that the total weight of each loaded skid is 1200 pounds and that the maximum allowable floor load is 280 lbs. per sq. ft.
   The MAXIMUM number of skids that can be stacked vertically without exceeding the MAXIMUM allowable floor load is

    A. 4 B. 5 C. 6 D. 7

7. Specifications which contain the term *slump test* would MOST likely refer to

   A. lumber   B. paint   C. concrete   D. water

8. Of the following sizes of copper conductors, the one which has the LEAST current-carrying capacity is _____ AWG.

   A. 000   B. 0   C. 8   D. 12

9. The size of a steel beam is shown on a steel drawing as W 8 x 15.
   In accordance with the latest edition of the Steel Construction Manual of the American Institute of Steel Construction, the number 8 in W 8 x 15 represents the beam's *approximate*

   A. depth
   B. flange thickness
   C. width
   D. web thickness

10. For expediting control functions such as work methods, planning, scheduling, and work measurement, EQUIPMENT RECORDS must contain specific data.
    Of the following, the data which is NOT usually indicated on an EQUIPMENT RECORD card is

    A. machinery and parts specifications numbers
    B. a breakdown history
    C. a preventive maintenance history
    D. salvage value on the open market

11. Refrigeration piping, valves, fittings, and related parts used in the construction and installation of refrigeration systems shall conform to the

    A. American Society of Mechanical Engineers Boiler and Pressure Vessel Code
    B. American Standards Association Code for Pressure Piping
    C. Pipe Fabrication Institute Standards
    D. Underwriters Laboratory Standards

12. The maintenance term *downtime* means MOST NEARLY the

    A. period of time in which a machine is out of service
    B. routine replacement of parts or materials to a piece of equipment
    C. labor required for clean-up of equipment to insure its proper operation
    D. maintenance work which is confined to checking, adjusting, and lubrication of equipment

13. A supplier quotes a list price of $172.00 less 15 and 10 percent for twelve tools.
    The ACTUAL cost for these twelve tools is MOST NEARLY

    A. $146   B. $132   C. $129   D. $112

14. Of the following colors of electrical conductor coverings, the one which indicates a conductor used SOLELY for grounding portable or fixed electrical equipment is

    A. blue   B. green   C. red   D. black

15. A *medium duty* type of scaffold is one on which the working load on the platform surface must NOT exceed _____ pounds per square foot.

    A. 50   B. 70   C. 90   D. 110

3 (#1)

16. Assume that a mechanic is using a powder-actuated tool and the cartridge misfires. According to recommended safe practices regarding a misfired cartridge, the FIRST course of action the mechanic should take is to

    A. place the misfired cartridge carefully into a metal container filled with water
    B. carefully reload the tool with the misfired cartridge and try it again
    C. immediately bury the misfired cartridge at least two feet in the ground
    D. remove the wadding from the misfired cartridge and empty the powder into a pail of sand

16._____

17. The ratings used in classifying fire resistant building construction materials are MOST frequently expressed in

    A. Btu's B. hours C. temperatures D. pounds

17._____

18. The only legible portion of the nameplate on a piece of equipment reads: *208 volts, 3 phase, 10 H.P.*
    This data would MOST NEARLY indicate that the piece of equipment is a(n)

    A. amplifier B. fixture ballast
    C. motor D. rectifier

18._____

19. Of the following items relating to the maintenance of roofs, the one which is of the LEAST value in a preventive maintenance program for roofs is knowledge of the

    A. roofing specifications B. application procedures
    C. process of deterioration D. frequency of rainstorms

19._____

20. In an oxyacetylene cutting outfit, the color of the hose that is connected to the oxygen cylinder is USUALLY

    A. white B. yellow C. red D. green

20._____

21. Assume that a welding generator is to be used to weld partitions made of 18 gauge steel. Of the following settings, the BEST one to use would be a _____ setting of voltage and a _____ setting of amperage.

    A. high; high B. high; low C. low; high D. low; low

21._____

22. According to the administrative code, when color marking is used, potable water lines shall be painted

    A. yellow B. blue C. red D. green

22._____

23. A set of mechanical plan drawings is drawn to a scale of 1/8" = 1 foot.
    If a length of pipe measures 15 7/16" on the drawing, the ACTUAL length of the pipe is _____ feet.

    A. 121.5 B. 122.5 C. 123.5 D. 124.5

23._____

24. A portion of a specification states: *Concrete, other than that placed under water, should be compacted and worked into place by spading or puddling.*
    The MAIN reason why *spading and puddling* is required is to

    A. insure that all water in the concrete mix is brought to the surface
    B. eliminate stone pockets and large bubbles of air

24._____

C. provide a means to obtain a spade full of concrete for test purposes
D. make allowances for *bleeding and segregation* of the concrete

25. Assume that the following statement appears in a construction contract: *Payment will be made for the number of pounds of bar reinforcement incorporated in the work as shown on the plans.*
    This type of contract is MOST likely

    A. cost plus   B. lump sum   C. subcontract   D. unit price

26. Partial payments to outside contractors are USUALLY based on the

    A. breakdown estimate submitted after the contract was signed
    B. actual cost of labor and material plus overhead and profit
    C. estimate of work completed which is generally submitted periodically
    D. estimate of material delivered to the job

27. Building contracts usually require that estimates for changes made in the field be submitted for approval before the work can start.
    The MAIN reason for this requirement is to

    A. make sure that the contractor understands the change
    B. discourage such changes
    C. keep the contractor honest
    D. enable the department to control its expenses

28. An *addendum* to contract specifications means MOST NEARLY

    A. a substantial completion payment to the contractor for work almost completed
    B. final acceptance of the work by authorities of all contract work still to be done
    C. additional contract provisions issued in writing by authorities prior to receipt of bids
    D. work other than that required by the contract at the time of its execution

29. Of the following terms, the one which is usually NOT used to describe the types of payments to outside contractors for work done is the _____ payment.

    A. partial payment   B. substantial completion
    C. final   D. surety

30. Of the following metals, the one which is a ferrous metal is

    A. cast iron   B. brass   C. bronze   D. babbit

31. Assume that you have assigned six mechanics to do a job that must be finished in four days. At the end of three days, your men have completed only two-thirds of the job. In order to complete the job on time and because the job is such that it cannot be speeded up, you should assign a MINIMUM of _____ extra men.

    A. 3   B. 4   C. 5   D. 6

32. Of the following traps, the one which is NORMALLY used to retain steam in a heating unit or piping is the _____ trap.

    A. P   B. running   C. float   D. bell

33. Of the following materials, the one which is a convenient and powerful adhesive for cementing tears in canvas jackets that are wrapped around warm pipe insulation is

    A. cylinder oil
    B. wheat paste
    C. water glass
    D. latex paint

34. Pipe chases should be provided with an access door PRIMARILY to provide means to

    A. replace piping lines
    B. either inspect or manipulate valves
    C. prevent condensate from forming on the pipes
    D. check the chase for possible structural defects

35. Electric power is measured in

    A. volts   B. amperes   C. watts   D. ohms

KEY (CORRECT ANSWERS)

1. D		16. A	
2. A		17. B	
3. B		18. C	
4. D		19. D	
5. C		20. D	
6. B		21. B	
7. C		22. D	
8. D		23. C	
9. A		24. B	
10. D		25. D	
11. B		26. C	
12. A		27. D	
13. B		28. C	
14. B		29. D	
15. A		30. A	

31. A
32. C
33. C
34. B
35. C

TEST 2

DIRECTIONS: Each question or incomplete statement is followed by several suggested answers or completions. Select the one that BEST answers the question or completes the statement. *PRINT THE LETTER OF THE CORRECT ANSWER IN THE SPACE AT THE RIGHT.*

1. The HIGHEST quality tools should

    A. always be bought
    B. never be bought
    C. be bought when they offer an overall advantage
    D. be bought only for foreman

2. Master keys should have no markings that will identify them as such.
   This statement is

    A. *false;* it would be impossible to keep records about them without such markings
    B. *true;* markings are subject to alteration and vandalization
    C. *false;* without such markings, they would be too lightly regarded by those to whom issued
    D. *true;* markings would only highlight their value to a potential wrongdoer

3. For a foreman to usually delay for a few weeks handling grievances his men make is a

    A. *poor* practice; it can affect the morale of the men
    B. *good* practice; it will discourage grievances
    C. *poor* practice; the causes of grievances usually disappear if action is delayed
    D. *good* practice; most employee grievances are not justified

4. Whenever an important change in procedure is contemplated, some foremen make a point of discussing the matter with their subordinates in order to get their viewpoint on the proposed change.
   In general, this practice is advisable MAINLY for the reason that

    A. subordinates can often see the effects of procedural changes more clearly than foremen
    B. the foreman has an opportunity to explain the advantages of the new procedure
    C. future changes will be welcomed if subordinates are kept informed
    D. participation in work planning helps to build a spirit of cooperation among employees

5. An estimate of employee morale could LEAST effectively be appraised by

    A. checking accident and absenteeism records
    B. determining the attitudes of employees toward their job
    C. examining the number of requests for emergency leaves of absence
    D. reviewing the number and nature of employee suggestions

6. Assume that you are a foreman and that a visitor at the job site asks you what your crew is doing.
   You should

A. respectfully decline to answer since all questions must be answered by the proper authority
B. answer as concisely as possible but discourage undue conversation
C. refer the man to your superiors
D. give the person complete details of the job

7. Cooperation can BEST be obtained from the general public by

   A. siding with them whenever they have a complaint
   B. sticking carefully to your work and ignoring everything else
   C. explaining the department's objectives and why the public must occasionally be temporarily inconvenienced
   D. listening politely to their complaints and telling them that the complaints will be forwarded to the main office

8. While you are working for the city, a man says to you that one of the rules of your job doesn't make sense and he gets mad.
   You should say to him

   A. Leave me alone so I can get my work done
   B. Everyone must follow the rules
   C. Let me tell you the reason for the rule
   D. I'm only doing my job so don't get mad at me

9. One approach to preparing written reports to superiors is to present first the conclusions and recommendations and then the data on which the conclusions and recommendations are based.
   The use of this approach is BEST justified when the

   A. data completely support the conclusions and recommendations
   B. superiors lack the specific training and experience required to understand and interpret the data
   C. data contain more information than is required for making the conclusions and recommendations
   D. superiors are more interested in the conclusions and recommendations than in the data

10. The MOST important reason why separate paragraphs might be used in writing a report is that this

    A. makes it easier to understand the report
    B. permits the report to be condensed
    C. gives a better appearance to the report
    D. prevents accidental elimination of important facts

11. On a drawing, the following standard cross-section represents MOST NEARLY

    A. sand   B. concrete   C. earth   D. rock

12. On a drawing, the following standard cross-section represents MOST NEARLY

    A. malleable iron B. steel
    C. bronze D. lead

13. On a piping plan drawing, the symbol represents a 90° _____ elbow.

    A. flanged B. screwed
    C. bell and spigot D. welded

14. On a drawing, the symbol represents

    A. stone B. steel C. glass D. wood

15. On a heating piping drawing, the symbol _____ represents piping.

    A. high-pressure steam B. medium-pressure steam
    C. low-pressure D. hot water supply

16. Of the following devices, the one that is LEAST frequently used to attach a piece of equipment to concrete or masonry walls is a(n)

    A. carriage bolt B. through bolt
    C. lag screw D. expansion bolt

17. A vapor barrier is usually installed in conjunction with

    A. drainage piping B. roof flashing
    C. building insulation D. wood sheathing

Questions 18-20.

DIRECTIONS: Questions 18 through 20 are to be answered in accordance with the following table

	Man Days Borough 1		Man Days Borough 2		Man Days Borough 3		Man Days Borough 4	
	Oct.	Nov.	Oct.	Nov.	Oct.	Nov.	Oct.	Nov.
Carpenter	70	100	35	180	145	205	120	85
Plumber	95	135	195	100	70	130	135	80
House Painter	90	90	120	80	85	85	95	195
Electrician	120	110	135	155	120	95	70	205
Blacksmith	125	145	60	180	205	145	80	125

18. In accordance with the above table, if the average daily pay of the five trades listed above is $47.50, the approximate labor cost of work done by the five trades during the month of October for Borough 1 is MOST NEARLY

    A. $22,800 B. $23,450 C. $23,750 D. $26,125

19. In accordance with the above table, the Borough which MOST NEARLY made up 22.4% of the total plumbing work force for the month of November is Borough

    A. 1   B. 2   C. 3   D. 4

20. In accordance with the above table, the average man days per month per Borough spent on electrical work for all Boroughs combined is MOST NEARLY

    A. 120   B. 126   C. 130   D. 136

21. Of the following percentages of carbon, the one that would indicate a medium carbon steel is

    A. 0.2%   B. 0.4%   C. 0.8%   D. 1.2%

22. A *screw pitch gage* measures only the

    A. looseness of threads
    B. tightness of threads
    C. number of threads per inch
    D. gage number

23. Assume that you are to make an inspection of a building to determine the need for painting.
    Of the following tools, the one which is LEAST needed to aid you in your inspection is a

    A. sharp penknife   B. putty knife
    C. lightweight tack hammer D. six-foot rule

24. A *slump test* for concrete is used MAINLY to measure the concrete's

    A. strength   B. consistency   C. flexibility   D. porosity

25. Specifications which contain the term *kiln dried* would MOST likely refer to

    A. asphalt shingles   B. brick veneer
    C. paint lacquer   D. lumber

26. In accordance with established jurisdictional work procedures among the trades, the person you would assign to replace a malfunctioning fire sprinkler head would be a

    A. plumber   B. laborer   C. housesmith   D. steamfitter

27. Of the following types of union shops, the one which is illegal under the Taft-Hartley Law is the _____ shop.

    A. closed   B. open
    C. union   D. union representative

28. Of the following types of contracts, the one that in city work would MOST likely be limited to emergency work *only* is

    A. lump-sum
    B. unit-price
    C. cost-plus
    D. partial cost-plus and lump-sum

29. Of the following qualifications of outside work contractors, the one which is the LEAST important requirement for determining eligible contractors is

    A. availability
    B. size of work force
    C. experience
    D. location of business

30. Of the following piping materials, the one that combines the physical strength of mild steel with the corrosion resistance of gray iron is

    A. grade A steel
    B. grey cast iron
    C. welded wrought iron
    D. ductile iron

31. Assume that a can of red lead paint needs to be thinned slightly. Of the following, the one that should be used is

    A. turpentine
    B. lacquer thinner
    C. water
    D. alcohol

32. Assume that a trench is 42" wide, 5' deep, and 100' long. If the unit price of excavating the trench is $35 per cubic yard, the cost of excavating the trench is MOST NEARLY

    A. $2,275   B. $5,110   C. $7,000   D. $21,000

33. Of the following uses, the one for which a bituminous compound would usually be used is to

    A. prevent corrosion of burled steel tanks
    B. increase the strength of concrete
    C. caulk water pipes
    D. paint inside wood columns

34. An electrical drawing is drawn to a scale of 1/4" = 1'.
    If a length of conduit on the drawing measures 7 3/8", the actual length of the conduit, in feet, is MOST NEARLY

    A. 7.5'   B. 15.5'   C. 22.5'   D. 29.5'

35. Of the following steam heating systems, the one that operates under both vacuum and low pressure conditions, without using a vacuum pump, is generally known as a _____ system.

    A. one pipe low pressure
    B. vacuum
    C. vapor
    D. high pressure

36. Of the following valve trim symbols, the one which designates a valve trim made of monel material is

    A. 8-18   B. NI-CU   C. SM   D. MI

37. A replacement part for a piece of equipment is to be made of S.A.E. 4047 steel. This material is MOST likely a _____ steel.

    A. wrought
    B. nickel
    C. chrome-vanadium
    D. molybdenum

38. A metallic underground water piping system is to be used as a means of grounding. Of the following statements concerning use of this system, the one that is MOST NEARLY CORRECT is that this use is

   A. not permitted
   B. permitted where available
   C. absolutely required
   D. permitted only in certain cases

39. For pipe sizes up to 8", schedule 40 pipe is identical to _____ pipe.

   A. standard
   B. extra strong
   C. double extra strong
   D. type M copper

40. Assume that a shop is undergoing a general housecleaning, and all excess unused materials have been removed. *Clean-up work,* as pertains to painting in this case, means MOST NEARLY

   A. a thorough two-coat paint job
   B. only that surface which was marred to be painted
   C. a one-coat job to *freshen things up*
   D. only that iron work is to be painted

41. The *United States Standard Gage* is used to measure sheet metal thicknesses of

   A. iron and steel
   B. aluminum
   C. copper
   D. tin

42. Headers and stretchers are used in the construction of

   A. floors   B. walls   C. ceilings   D. roofs

Questions 43-44.

DIRECTIONS: Questions 43 and 44, inclusive, are to be answered in accordance with the following paragraph.

For cast iron pipe lines, the middle ring or sleeve shall have <u>beveled</u> ends and shall be high quality cast iron. The middle ring shall have a minimum wall thickness of 3/8" for pipe up to 8", 7/16" for pipe 10" to 30", and 1/2" for pipe over 30", nominal diameter. Minimum length of middle ring shall be 5" for pipe up to 10", 6" for pipe 10" to 30", and 10" for pipe 30" nominal diameter and larger. The middle ring shall not have a center pipe stop, unless otherwise specified.

43. As used in the above paragraph, the word *beveled* means MOST NEARLY

   A. straight   B. slanted   C. curved   D. rounded

44. In accordance with the above paragraph, the middle ring of a 24" nominal diameter pipe would have a minimum wall thickness and length of _____ thick and _____ long.

   A. 3/8"; 5"   B. 3/8"; 6"   C. 7/16"; 6"   D. 1/2"; 6"

7 (#2)

45. A work order is NOT usually issued for which one of the following jobs:

    A. Repairing wood door frames
    B. Taking daily inventory
    C. Installing electric switches in maintenance shop
    D. Repairing a number of valves in boiler room

46. Of the following statements, the one which usually does NOT pertain to preventative maintenance programs is

    A. periodic inspection of facilities
    B. lubrication of equipment
    C. minor repair of equipment
    D. complete replacement of deteriorated equipment

Questions 47-50.

DIRECTIONS: Questions 47 through 50, inclusive, are based on the sketch of metal sheet shown below. (Sketch not to scale.)

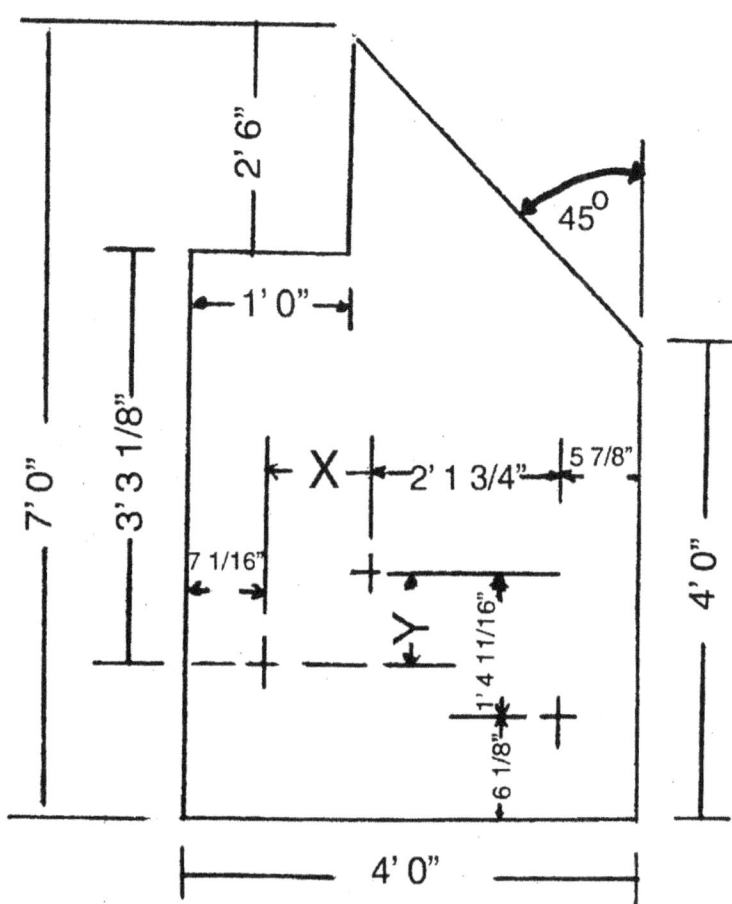

47. From the above sketch, the distance marked X is MOST NEARLY

    A. 5 1/4"   B. 6 5/16"   C. 7 1/8"   D. 9 5/16"

48. From the above sketch, the distance marked Y is MOST NEARLY   48._____

    A. 5 11/16"   B. 6 3/16"   C. 7 5/16"   D. 8 11/16"

49. In reference to the above sketch, if each piece is made from a rectangular piece of metal   49._____
    measuring 4' x 7', the percent of waste material is MOST NEARLY

    A. 10%   B. 15%   C. 25%   D. 30%

50. In reference to the above sketch, if the metal is 1/4" thick and weighs 144 pounds per   50._____
    cubic foot, the net weight of one piece would be MOST NEARLY _____ pounds.

    A. 51   B. 63   C. 75   D. 749

KEY (CORRECT ANSWERS)

1.	C	11.	A	21.	B	31.	A	41.	A
2.	D	12.	C	22.	C	32.	A	42.	B
3.	A	13.	A	23.	D	33.	A	43.	B
4.	D	14.	D	24.	B	34.	D	44.	C
5.	C	15.	B	25.	D	35.	C	45.	B
6.	B	16.	A	26.	D	36.	B	46.	D
7.	C	17.	C	27.	A	37.	D	47.	D
8.	C	18.	C	28.	C	38.	B	48.	D
9.	D	19.	B	29.	D	39.	A	49.	C
10.	A	20.	B	30.	D	40.	C	50.	B

EXAMINATION SECTION
TEST 1

DIRECTIONS: Each question or incomplete statement is followed by several suggested answers or completions. Select the one that BEST answers the question or completes the statement. *PRINT THE LETTER OF THE CORRECT ANSWER IN THE SPACE AT THE RIGHT.*

1. A maintenance man complains to you that he is getting all the boring jobs to do. You check and find that his complaint has no basis in fact.
   The one of the following which is the MOST likely reason why the maintenance man made such a claim is that he

   A. wants to get even with the supervisor
   B. lives in a world of fantasy
   C. believes the injustice to be real
   D. is jealous of other workers

   1.____

2. When on preliminary review of a mechanic's written grievance you feel the grievance to be unfounded, the FIRST step you should take is to

   A. show the mechanic where he is wrong
   B. check carefully to find out why the mechanic thinks that way
   C. try to humor the mechanic out of it
   D. tell the mechanic to stop complaining

   2.____

3. Assume that you decide to hold a private meeting with one of your mechanics who has a drinking problem that is affecting his work.
   At the meeting, the BEST way for you to handle this situation is to

   A. tell the mechanic off and then listen to what he has to say
   B. criticize the mechanic's behavior to get him to *open up* in order to help him correct his problem quickly
   C. try to get the mechanic to recognize his problem and find ways to solve it
   D. limit the discussion to matters concerning only the problem and look for immediate results

   3.____

4. The one of the following which is a generally accepted guide in criticizing a subordinate EFFECTIVELY is to

   A. criticize the improper act, not the individual
   B. put the listener on the defensive
   C. make the criticism general instead of specific
   D. correct the personality, not the situation

   4.____

5. The one of the following disciplinary methods by which you are MOST likely to be successful in getting a problem employee to improve his behavior is when you

   A. discipline the employee in front of others
   B. consider the matter to be ended after the disciplining
   C. give the exact same discipline no matter how serious the wrongdoing
   D. make an example of the employee

   5.____

6. Of the following statements, the one that is MOST applicable to a disciplinary situation is that discipline should be

   A. used after a cooling-off period
   B. identical for all employees
   C. consistent with the violation
   D. based on personal feelings

7. The one of the following approaches that is MOST important for you to take in evaluating a mechanic in order to increase his work productivity is to

   A. first have him evaluate his own performance
   B. meet with him to discuss how he is doing and what is expected on the job
   C. send him a copy of your evaluation of his work performance and give him the opportunity to submit written comments
   D. express in writing your appreciation of his work

8. Assume that you say to one of the mechanics, *Jim, that job you turned out today was top-notch. I didn't think you could do so well with the kind of material you had to work with.*
   This statement BEST describes an example of your

   A. recognition of the man's work
   B. disrespect for the man's feelings
   C. personal favoritism of the man
   D. constructive criticism of the man's work

9. In general, the OUTSTANDING characteristic of employees over 50 years of age is their

   A. resistance   B. endurance
   C. wisdom   D. job stability

10. You should be interested in the morale of your men because morale is MOST often associated with

    A. mechanization   B. automation
    C. production   D. seniority regulations

11. Assume that the maintenance work order system is about to be changed. Your workers would MOST likely show the LEAST resistance to this change if you

    A. downgrade the old maintenance work order system
    B. tell your workers how the change will benefit them
    C. post the notice of the change on the bulletin board
    D. tell the workers how the change will benefit management

12. Of the following, the BEST way to motivate a newly appointed mechanic is to

    A. explain the meaning of each assignment
    B. make the work more physically demanding
    C. test the mechanic's ability
    D. use as much authority as possible

13. The one of the following which is the LEAST important reason for giving employees information concerning policy changes which will affect them is that employees should know

    A. why the change is being made
    B. who will be affected by the change
    C. when the change will go into effect
    D. how much savings will be made by the change

14. A foreman who knows how to handle his men will MOST likely get them to produce more by treating them

    A. alike
    B. as individuals
    C. on a casual basis
    D. as a group

15. Of the following items, the one that a supervisor has the MOST right to expect from his employees is

    A. liking the job
    B. a fair day's work
    C. equal skill of all mechanics
    D. perfection

16. The one of the following which is the BEST practice for you to follow in handling a dispute between the workers is to

    A. side with one of the workers so as to end the dispute quickly
    B. pay no attention to the dispute and let the workers settle it themselves
    C. listen to each worker's story of the dispute and then decide how to settle it
    D. discuss the dispute with other workers and then decide how to settle it

17. You are likely to run into an employee morale problem when assigning a dirty job that comes up often.
    Of the following, the BEST method of assigning this work is to

    A. rotate this assignment
    B. assign it to the fastest worker
    C. assign it by seniority
    D. assign it to the least skilled worker

18. Of the following, the one that is generally regarded as the BEST aid to high work productivity of subordinates is a supervisor's skill in

    A. record keeping
    B. technical work
    C. setting up rules and regulations
    D. human relations

19. The BEST way to help a mechanic who comes to you for advice on a personal problem is to

    A. listen to the worker's problem without passing judgment
    B. tell the worker to forget about the problem and to stop letting it interfere with his work
    C. talk about your own personal problems to the worker
    D. mind your own business and leave the worker alone

20. You are in charge of the maintenance shop and have learned that within the next two weeks the maintenance shop will be moved to a new location on the plant grounds, but you have not learned why this move is taking place. Assume that you have decided not to keep this information from your mechanics until the reason is known but to inform them of this matter now.
Of the following, which one is the BEST argument that can be made regarding your decision?

    A. *Acceptable;* because although the reason is not now known, the mechanics will eventually find out about the move
    B. *Unacceptable;* because the mechanics do not know at this time the reason for the move and this will cause anxiety on their part
    C. *Acceptable*; because the mechanics will be affected by the move and they should be told what is happening
    D. *Unacceptable;* because the mechanics' advance knowledge of the move will tend to slow down their work output

20.____

21. Of the following, the FIRST action for a foreman to take in making a decision is to

    A. get all the facts
    B. develop alternate solutions
    C. get opinions of others
    D. know the results in advance

21.____

22. Assume that you have just been promoted to foreman.
Of the following, the BEST practice to follow regarding your previous experience at the mechanic's level is to

    A. continue to fraternize with your old friends
    B. use this experience to better understand those who now work for you
    C. use your old connections to keep top management informed of mechanics' views
    D. forget the mechanics' points of view

22.____

23. You have decided to hold regular group discussions with your subordinates on various aspects of their duties.
Of the following methods you might use to begin such a program, the one which is likely to be MOST productive is to

    A. express your own ideas and persuade the group to accept them
    B. save time and cover more ground by asking questions calling for yes or no answers
    C. propose to the group a general plan of action rather than specific ideas carefully worked out
    D. provide an informal atmosphere for the exchange of ideas

23.____

24. The principle of learning by which a foreman might get the BEST results in training his subordinates is:

    A. Letting the learner discover and correct his own mistakes
    B. Teaching the most technical part of the work first
    C. Teaching all parts of the work during the first training session
    D. Getting the learner to use as many of his five senses as possible

24.____

25. A new mechanic is to be trained to do an involved operation containing several steps of varying difficulty. This mechanic will MOST likely learn the operation more quickly if he is taught

    A. each step in its proper order
    B. the hardest steps first
    C. the easiest steps first
    D. first the steps that do not require tools

25._____

KEY (CORRECT ANSWERS)

1. C	11. B
2. B	12. A
3. C	13. D
4. A	14. B
5. B	15. B
6. C	16. C
7. B	17. A
8. A	18. D
9. D	19. A
10. C	20. C

21. A
22. B
23. D
24. D
25. C

TEST 2

DIRECTIONS: Each question or incomplete statement is followed by several suggested answers or completions. Select the one that BEST answers the question or completes the statement. *PRINT THE LETTER OF THE CORRECT ANSWER IN THE SPACE AT THE RIGHT.*

1. The one of the following job situations in which it is better to give a written order than an oral order is when

   A. the job involves many details
   B. you can check the job's progress easily
   C. the job is repetitive in nature
   D. there is an emergency

   1.____

2. Which one of the following serves as the BEST guideline for you to follow for effective written reports?
   Keep sentences

   A. short and limit sentences to one thought
   B. short and use as many thoughts as possible
   C. long and limit sentences to one thought
   D. long and use as many thoughts as possible

   2.____

3. Of the following, the BEST reason why a foreman generally should not do the work of an individual mechanic is that

   A. the shop's production figures will not be accurate
   B. a foreman is paid to supervise
   C. the foreman must maintain his authority
   D. the employee may become self-conscious

   3.____

4. One method by which a foreman might prepare written reports to management is to begin with the conclusions, results, or summary and to follow this with the supporting data.
   The BEST reason why management may prefer this form of report is because

   A. management lacks the specific training to understand the data
   B. the data completely supports the conclusions
   C. time is saved by getting to the conclusions of the report first
   D. the data contains all the information that is required for making the conclusions

   4.____

5. Forms used for time records and work orders are important to the work of a foreman PRIMARILY because they give him

   A. the knowledge of and familiarity with work operations
   B. the means of control of personnel, material, or job costs
   C. the means for communicating with other workers
   D. a useful method for making filing procedures easier

   5.____

6. The one of the following which is the MOST important factor in determining the number of employees you can effectively supervise is the

    A. type of work to be performed
    B. priority of the work to be performed
    C. salary level of the workers
    D. ratio of permanent employees to temporary employees

6._____

7. Of the following, you will be MOST productive in carrying out your supervisory responsibilities if you

    A. are capable of doing the same work as your mechanics
    B. meet with your mechanics frequently
    C. are very friendly with your mechanics
    D. get work done through your mechanics

7._____

8. You have been asked to prepare the annual budget for your maintenance shop.
The one of the following which is the FIRST step you should take in preparing this budget is to determine the

    A. amount of maintenance work which is scheduled for the shop
    B. time it takes for a specific unit of work to be completed
    C. current workload of each employee in the shop
    D. policies and procedures of the shop's operations

8._____

9. When determining the amount of work you expect a group of mechanics to perform in a given time, the BEST procedure for you to follow should be to

    A. aim for a higher level of production than that of the most productive worker
    B. stay at the present production level
    C. set general instead of specific goals
    D. let workers participate in the determination whenever possible

9._____

10. You have been asked to set next year's performance goals concerning the ratio of jobs completed on schedule to total jobs worked. A review of last year's record shows that the workers completed their jobs on schedule 85% of the time, with the best ones showing an on-time ratio of 92% and the poorest ones showing an on-time ratio of 65%.
Using these facts in line with generally accepted goal-setting practices, you should set a performance ratio for the next year on the basis of _____ average with a _____ minimum acceptable for any employee.

    A. 85%; 65%   B. 85%; 70%   C. 90%; 65%   D. 90%; 70%

10._____

11. It is important for you to be able to identify the critical parts of a large project such as the remodeling of your maintenance shop.
The one of the following which is the BEST reason why this is important is that it may

    A. help you to set up good communications between you and your workers
    B. give you a better understanding of the purpose of the project
    C. give you control over the time and cost involved in the project
    D. help you to determine who are your most productive workers

11._____

12. When doing work planning for your shop, the factor that you should normally consider LAST among the following is knowing your

    A. major objectives
    B. record keeping system
    C. minor objectives
    D. priorities

13. You have the responsibility for ordering all materials for your maintenance shop. A listing of materials needed for the operations of your shop is long overdue. You realize that you are unable to find time to take care of the inventory personally because of a high priority project you have been working on which has been taking all of your time. You do not know when you will be finished with the project.
    The BEST of the following courses of action to take in handling this inventory matter is to

    A. request that you be taken off the project immediately so that you may take care of the inventory
    B. complete your high priority project and then do the inventory yourself
    C. volunteer to work overtime so that you may complete the inventory while continuing with the project
    D. assign the inventory work to a competent subordinate

14. You have the authority and responsibility for seeing that proper records are kept in your shop. Assume that you decide to delegate to a records clerk the responsibility for collecting the time sheets and the authority to make changes on the time sheets to correct the information when necessary.
    Of the following, which one is the BEST argument that can be made regarding your decision?

    A. *Unacceptable*; because you can delegate only your responsibility but none of your authority to the records clerk
    B. *Acceptable*; because you can delegate some of your authority and some of your responsibility to the records clerk
    C. *Unacceptable;* because you can delegate only your authority but none of your responsibility to the records clerk
    D. *Acceptable;* because you can delegate all your responsibility and all your authority to the records clerk

15. You will LEAST likely be able to do an effective job of controlling operating costs if you

    A. eliminate idle time
    B. reduce absenteeism
    C. raise your budget
    D. combine work operations

16. Of the following actions, the one which is LEAST likely to help in carrying out your responsibilities of looking after the interests of your workers is to

    A. crack down on your workers when necessary
    B. let your workers know that you support company policy
    C. prevent the transfers of your workers
    D. back up your workers in a controversy

17. The term *accountability*, as used in management of supervision, means MOST NEARLY

    A. responsibility for results
    B. record keeping
    C. bookkeeping systems
    D. inventory control

18. Assume that you have been unable to convince an employee of the seriousness of his poor attendance record by talking to him.
    The one of the following which is the BEST course of action for you to take is to

    A. keep talking to the employee
    B. recommend that a written warning be given
    C. consider transferring the employee to another work location
    D. recommend that the employee be fired

19. When delegating work to a subordinate foreman, you should NOT

    A. delegate the right to make any decisions
    B. be interested in the results of the work, but in the method of doing the work
    C. delegate any work that you can do better than your subordinate
    D. give up your final responsibility for the work

20. Of the following statements, the BEST reason why proper scheduling of maintenance work is important is that it

    A. eliminates the need for individual job work orders
    B. classifies job skills in accordance with performance
    C. minimizes lost time in performing any maintenance job
    D. determines needed repairs in various locations

21. Of the following factors, the one which is of LEAST importance in determining the number of subordinates that an individual should be assigned to supervise is the

    A. nature of the work being supervised
    B. qualifications of the individual as a supervisor
    C. capabilities of the subordinates
    D. lines of promotion for the subordinates

22. Suppose that a large number of semi-literate residents of this city have been requesting the assistance of your department. You are asked to prepare a form which these applicants will be required to fill out before their requests will be considered.
    In view of these facts, the one of the following factors to which you should give the GREATEST amount of consideration in preparing this form is the

    A. size of the form
    B. sequence of the information asked for on the form
    C. level of difficulty of the language used in the form
    D. number of times which the form will have to be reviewed

23. A budget is a plan whereby a goal is set for future operations. It affords a medium for comparing actual expenditures with planned expenditures.
    The one of the following which is the MOST accurate statement on the basis of this statement is that

    A. the budget serves as an accurate measure of past as well as future expenditures
    B. the budget presents an estimate of expenditures to be made in the future
    C. budget estimates should be based upon past budget requirements
    D. planned expenditures usually fall short of actual expenditures

24. A foreman who is familiar with modern management principles should know that the one of the following requirements of an administrator which is LEAST important is his ability to

    A. coordinate work
    B. plan, organize, and direct the work under his control
    C. cooperate with others
    D. perform the duties of the employees under his jurisdiction

25. The one of the following which should be considered the LEAST important objective of the service rating system is to

    A. rate the employees on the basis of their potential abilities
    B. establish a basis for assigning employees to special types of work
    C. provide a means of recognizing superior work performance
    D. reveal the need for training as well as the effectiveness of a training program

KEY (CORRECT ANSWERS)

1.	A	11.	C
2.	A	12.	B
3.	B	13.	D
4.	C	14.	B
5.	B	15.	C
6.	A	16.	C
7.	D	17.	A
8.	A	18.	B
9.	D	19.	D
10.	D	20.	C

21. D
22. C
23. B
24. D
25. A

EXAMINATION SECTION
TEST 1

DIRECTIONS: Each question or incomplete statement is followed by several suggested answers or completions. Select the one that BEST answers the question or completes the statement. *PRINT THE LETTER OF THE CORRECT ANSWER IN THE SPACE AT THE RIGHT.*

1. Which of the following types of estimates is considered BEST for estimating the total cost of a job?

    A. Unit cost estimate
    B. Lump-sum amount
    C. Cost-per-square-foot estimate
    D. Quantity survey

2. The scale of a typical set of architectural drawings uses _____ to represent 1 foot.

    A. 1/8"   B. 1/4"   C. 1/2"   D. 1"

3. A *square* in construction terms is an area of roofing that is _____ square feet.

    A. 40   B. 75   C. 100   D. 120

4. A _____ is represented by the mechanical symbol

    A. liquid pump
    B. water closet, flush valve
    C. compressor
    D. duct volume damper

5. Typically, a mud sill is bolted to a concrete foundation at intervals of _____ inches.

    A. 12-18   B. 18-36   C. 36-48   D. 48-60

6. For how many hours should an *A label* fire door be able to withstand continuous fire exposure?

    A. 3/4   B. 1   C. 1 1/2   D. 3

7. The current-carrying capacity of an electric device is USUALLY expressed in terms of

    A. voltage   B. amperage   C. gauge   D. resistance

8. Construction drawings show *quantities* via each of the following EXCEPT

    A. plans
    B. sections
    C. specifications
    D. details

9. What type of window consists of two or more sashes, one or more of which are moved horizontally?

    A. Transom
    B. Sliding
    C. Casement
    D. Double-hung

10. If boards are to be used for floor sheathing, the amount for cut-off ends and waste should be figured as _____% more than the floor space area to be sheathed.

    A. 5   B. 10   C. 20   D. 30

11. Grade B sheet glass can be used for glazing up to _____ square feet of area.

    A. 10   B. 16   C. 24   D. 30

12. What is generally considered to be the MAXIMUM roof pitch allowable for the use of roll roofing?
    _____ in 12.

    A. 2   B. 4   C. 6   D. 8

13. What is represented by the architectural symbol shown at the right?

    A. Stone concrete
    B. Cinder concrete
    C. Gravel
    D. Plaster

14. For estimating purposes, construction sound control methods are divided into each of the following major types EXCEPT

    A. construction with spaced studs and/or layered wall board
    B. absorbing material applied over wall or ceiling surfaces
    C. suspended ceilings
    D. sound-dampening floor covering

15. What is used to cover the ends of rafters in a cornice construction?

    A. Fascia
    B. Hips
    C. Shears
    D. Butt joints

16. Which of the following steps in a grading-quantity estimation would be performed FIRST?

    A. Determine approximate finish grade
    B. Calculate difference between cut and fill
    C. Estimate elevation of grid corners from contours
    D. Average the elevation of each grid square

17. What amount of masonry should a bricklayer and tender be able to install in an average work day?

    A. 50 square feet
    B. 100 square feet
    C. 50 cubic feet
    D. 100 linear feet

18. The time required for the placement labor and staking of slab-on-grade foundation forms should be calculated at APPROXIMATELY _____ hour(s) for 100 linear feet.

    A. 1/2   B. 1   C. 2 1/2   D. 3 1/2

19. What is represented by the mechanical symbol shown at the right?

    A. Wall air outlet
    B. Clean out
    C. Duct volume damper
    D. Blower

20. What is the term for a steel pipe filled with concrete and used as a beam support? 20.____

    A. Bearing column B. Platform frame
    C. Lally column   D. Soffit

21. Which of the following types of wood windows would be MOST expensive to install? 21.____

    A. Awning   B. Casement
    C. Double-hung D. Horizontal sliding

22. A workman is installing 3 1/2-inch-thick batts of R-11 fiberglass insulation. 22.____
    About how many square feet will the workman be able to install in a typical work day?

    A. 300-500   B. 650-1000   C. 1200-1500   D. 1750-2000

23. What is represented by the architectural symbol shown at the right? 23.____

    A. Cast iron B. Aluminum
    C. Steel   D. Brick

24. Most rafters are spaced _____ inches apart. 24.____

    A. 18   B. 24   C. 36   D. 48

25. What is the dividing strip within a window assembly that separates the various panes of glass? 25.____

    A. Muntin   B. Sash   C. Bunting   D. Mullion

KEY (CORRECT ANSWERS)

1. D	11. B
2. B	12. B
3. C	13. B
4. A	14. D
5. D	15. A
6. D	16. C
7. B	17. B
8. C	18. D
9. B	19. C
10. C	20. C

21. C
22. C
23. C
24. B
25. A

TEST 2

DIRECTIONS: Each question or incomplete statement is followed by several suggested answers or completions. Select the one that BEST answers the question or completes the statement. *PRINT THE LETTER OF THE CORRECT ANSWER IN THE SPACE AT THE RIGHT.*

1. What type of brick masonry unit is represented by the drawing shown at the right?
   A. Norman
   B. Economy
   C. King Norman
   D. Double

   1.___

2. The typical thickness of asphalt paving, applied over a gravel base course, is

   A. 1/2-2"   B. 1-3"   C. 2-5"   D. 3-7"

   2.___

3. Which of the following waterproofing materials is LEAST expensive?

   A. Two-ply polyethylene (.002")
   B. Sprayed-on bituminous coating
   C. Two-ply felt membrane
   D. Elastomeric waterproofing (1/32")

   3.___

4. Each of the following structures must always be included in an estimate if a *hip* roof is shown on drawings EXCEPT

   A. box cornice   B. collar beam
   C. fascia   D. solid sheathing

   4.___

5. What is represented by the electrical symbol shown at the right?

   A. Special purpose outlet   B. Transformer
   C. Paging system   D. Telephone

   5.___

6. The edge of a roof at the end of a building is called a

   A. sill   B. cornice   C. frieze   D. rake

   6.___

7. According to established finish-designation standards, which of the following finish materials would be ranked at the HIGHEST grade?

   A. White bronze   B. Bright bronze
   C. Nickel-plated   D. Cadmium-plated

   7.___

8. What is represented by the electrical symbol shown at the right?

   A. Duplex receptacle
   B. Call system
   C. Wall bracket light fixture
   D. Ceiling light fixture

   8.___

88

9. How many board-feet of rafters should two carpenters be able to install in a typical work day?   9.____

    A. 250   B. 500   C. 800   D. 1200

10. The valve at the LOWEST point of a water system is the   10.____

    A. drain cock   B. globe valve
    C. check valve   D. ball cock

11. When purchasing siding, what percentage of the material should typically be calculated as waste?   11.____

    A. 10%   B. 15%   C. 25%   D. 35%

12. Which of the following is considered a *variable* overhead cost?   12.____

    A. Business permit   B. Storage space
    C. Job permit   D. Office utilities

13. What is the MOST commonly used paint base for use in kitchens and baths?   13.____

    A. Oil latex   B. Oleoresin
    C. Urethane   D. Alkyd enamel

14. Approximately how many linear feet of caulking material would be required for each door/window opening?   14.____

    A. 5-10   B. 12-15   C. 18-20   D. 22-28

15. What type of window is hinged at the side and opens outward from the opposite edge?   15.____

    A. Awning   B. Casement   C. Storm   D. Sliding

16. Approximately how many square feet of particle board floor underlayment can be installed by a crew in a normal work day?   16.____

    A. 250   B. 750   C. 1200   D. 1500

17. What is represented by the architectural symbol shown at the right?   17.____

    A. Earth   B. Sand   C. Plaster   D. Fire brick

18. Approximately how many linear feet of drywall tape will be required for 1000 square feet of area?   18.____

    A. 250   B. 400   C. 750   D. 1000

19. Which type of paving material can typically be applied MOST quickly?   19.____

    A. Asphalt   B. Concrete, no curbs
    C. Random flagstone   D. Concrete sidewalk

20. Approximately how many square feet of door and window surfaces should a painter be able to cover in one hour?   20.____

    A. 50   B. 75   C. 125   D. 175

21. What is the term for the thin coat of plaster applied to masonry or concrete walls to obtain a watertight or smooth surface?   21.____

    A. Plate   B. Laminate   C. Parging   D. Cripple

22. For estimating the labor cost of the installation of countertops and sink splashes, the typical tile labor time should be multiplied by   22.____

    A. 1/2   B. 2   C. 3   D. 4

23. In most retail stores, the markup for overhead profit is _____% over the wholesale cost of the material.   23.____

    A. 7-10   B. 12-25   C. 33-50   D. 40-60

24. When making wall covering estimates, the general practice is to add _____% to the cost of materials to account for waste and pattern matching.   24.____

    A. 10   B. 20   C. 35   D. 45

25. The underside of a cornice, beam, or any other material is known as a   25.____

    A. screed   B. section   C. truss   D. soffit

KEY (CORRECT ANSWERS)

1.	C	11.	A
2.	B	12.	C
3.	A	13.	D
4.	B	14.	C
5.	B	15.	B
6.	D	16.	D
7.	A	17.	A
8.	D	18.	B
9.	C	19.	A
10.	A	20.	C
21.	C		
22.	C		
23.	C		
24.	B		
25.	D		

TEST 3

DIRECTIONS: Each question or incomplete statement is followed by several suggested answers or completions. Select the one that BEST answers the question or completes the statement. *PRINT THE LETTER OF THE CORRECT ANSWER IN THE SPACE AT THE RIGHT.*

1. Approximately how many square feet of 4 1/4" x 4 1/4" glazed wall tile, applied with the adhesive-set method, can be applied in an average work day?   1.____

   A. 60　　　　B. 130　　　　C. 175　　　　D. 220

2. Which of the following would NOT be a typical R-value for fiberglass roll insulation material?   2.____

   A. R-8　　　　B. R-11　　　　C. R-23　　　　D. R-30

3. What is represented by the electrical symbol shown at the right?   3.____

   A. Signal push button　　　　B. Fluorescent light fixture
   C. Radio outlet　　　　D. Street light and bracket

4. Generally, finishing hardware costs will be a MAXIMUM of _____% of the total job cost.   4.____

   A. .5　　　　B. 1　　　　C. 3　　　　D. 7

5. Built-up roofs are MOST often made from   5.____

   A. saturated felt　　　　B. tarpaper shingles
   C. wood shake　　　　D. tile

6. What is represented by the architectural symbol shown at the right?   6.____

   A. Cut stone　　　　B. Concrete block
   C. Rubble stone　　　　D. Brick

7. Most tubs, toilets, sinks, and lavatories require an average of _____ hours labor for the installation of rough plumbing.   7.____

   A. 3　　　　B. 5　　　　C. 7　　　　D. 9

8. What is the term for the inclined members of a stair that support the other members?   8.____

   A. Stringers　　　　B. Slopes　　　　C. Slumps　　　　D. Risers

9. Approximately how many square yards of diamond metal lath wall support can be installed in a typical work day?   9.____

   A. 30-40　　　　B. 50-60　　　　C. 75-85　　　　D. 85-100

10. What type of concrete masonry unit is represented by the drawing shown at the right?   10.____
    A. Double corner
    B. Soffit floor
    C. Corner
    D. Half cut header

11. Which of the following diameters would be MOST typical for a caisson hole?

    A. 12-24"   B. 30-36"   C. 40-48"   D. 60-72"

12. One bundle of six gypsum lath will cover an area of _____ square feet of wall space.

    A. 18   B. 32   C. 48   D. 64

13. The estimate for cost of forms typically relies on

    A. surface contact feet
    B. cubic feet of foundation material
    C. material used as studs
    D. linear feet of forms

14. What is represented by the architectural symbol shown at the right?

    A. Batted insulation   B. Vertical siding
    C. Concrete block   D. Ceramic tile

15. Approximately how many square feet of finish plywood siding can be installed by two carpenters in a typical work day?

    A. 200   B. 650   C. 850   D. 1200

16. After construction has begun, various fabricated items may require drawings that will indicate the exact size, shape, and material that the fabrication will have.
    These drawings are called

    A. detail drawings   B. shop drawings
    C. diagrams   D. specifications

17. How many bundles of roofing shakes, installed at 10" exposure, would be required to cover one square of roof area?

    A. 1   B. 3   C. 5   D. 7

18. What type of labor will normally be calculated for waterproofing work?

    A. Carpentry   B. Roofing
    C. Common labor   D. Tile

19. Which of the following is NOT generally classified as *rough* plumbing?

    A. Hot water line   B. Tub fixture
    C. Vent stack   D. Gas piping

20. Approximately how many square feet of 20-year bonded flat roofing can be installed by a crew in an average work day?

    A. 400-600   B. 750-1000
    C. 1200-1600   D. 1800-2000

21. Approximately how many hours of labor will be required for the machine sanding of 1000 square feet of unfinished wood strip flooring?

    A. 1/2   B. 1   C. 3   D. 4 1/2

22. What is represented by the mechanical symbol —⋈— shown at the right? 22.____

    A. Diaphragm valve   B. Lock and shield valve
    C. Gate valve   D. Check valve

23. Approximately how many linear feet of mud sill should a 2-person crew be able to install in a typical work day? 23.____

    A. 50-100   B. 150-250   C. 250-300   D. 350-400

24. When calculating the area of a gabled roof, the estimator should remember to multiply the initial figure by 24.____

    A. 1/4   B. 1/2   C. 2   D. 4

25. The calculation of the square-foot area of a building includes the area of the 25.____

    A. internal face   B. basement
    C. attic   D. external face

KEY (CORRECT ANSWERS)

1.	C	11.	B
2.	A	12.	B
3.	B	13.	A
4.	C	14.	A
5.	A	15.	B
6.	B	16.	B
7.	B	17.	C
8.	A	18.	B
9.	B	19.	B
10.	C	20.	D

21. B
22. C
23. C
24. C
25. D

EXAMINATION SECTION
TEST 1

DIRECTIONS: Each question or incomplete statement is followed by several suggested answers or completions. Select the one that BEST answers the question or completes the statement. *PRINT THE LETTER OF THE CORRECT ANSWER IN THE SPACE AT THE RIGHT.*

1. Of the following, the one MOST important quality required of a good supervisor is
   A. ambition   B. leadership   C. friendliness   D. popularity

   1._____

2. It is often said that a supervisor can delegate authority but never responsibility. This means MOST NEARLY that
   A. a supervisor must do his own work if he expects it to be done properly
   B. a supervisor can assign someone else to do his work, but in the last analysis, the supervisor himself must take the blame for any actions followed
   C. authority and responsibility are two separate things that cannot be borne by the same person
   D. it is better for a supervisor never to delegate his authority

   2._____

3. One of your men who is a habitual complainer asks you to grant him a minor privilege.
   Before granting or denying such a request, you should consider
   A. the merits of the case
   B. that it is good for group morale to grant a request of this nature
   C. the man's seniority
   D. that to deny such a request will lower your standing with the men

   3._____

4. A supervisory practice on the part of a foreman which is MOST likely to lead to confusion and inefficiency is for him to
   A. give orders verbally directly to the man assigned to the job
   B. issue orders only in writing
   C. follow up his orders after issuing them
   D. relay his orders to the men through co-workers

   4._____

5. It would be POOR supervision on a foreman's part if he
   A. asked an experienced maintainer for his opinion on the method of doing a special job
   B. make it a policy to avoid criticizing a man in front of his co-workers
   C. consulted his assistant supervisor on unusual problems
   D. allowed a cooling-off period of several days before giving one of his men a deserved reprimand

   5._____

2 (#1)

6. Of the following behavior characteristics of a supervisor, the one that is MOST likely to lower the morale of the men he supervises is
   A. diligence
   B. favoritism
   C. punctuality
   D. thoroughness

   6.____

7. Of the following, the BEST method of getting an employee who is not working up to his capacity to produce more work is to
   A. have another employee criticize his production
   B. privately criticize his production but encourage him to produce more
   C. criticize his production before his associates
   D. criticize his production and threaten to fire him

   7.____

8. Of the following, the BEST thing for a supervisor to do when a subordinate has done a very good job is to
   A. tell him to take it easy
   B. praise his work
   C. reduce his workload
   D. say nothing because he may become conceited

   8.____

9. Your orders to your crew are MOST likely to be followed if you
   A. explain the reasons for these orders
   B. warn that all violators will be punished
   C. promise easy assignments to those who follow these orders best
   D. say that they are for the good of the department

   9.____

10. In order to be a good supervisor, you should
    A. impress upon your men that you demand perfection in their work at all times
    B. avoid being blamed for your crew's mistakes
    C. impress your superior with your ability
    D. see to it that your men get what they are entitled to

    10.____

11. In giving instructions to a crew, you should
    A. speak in as loud a tone as possible
    B. speak in a coaxing, persuasive manner
    C. speak quietly, clearly, and courteously
    D. always use the word *please* when giving instructions

    11.____

12. Of the following factors, the one which is LEAST important in evaluating an employee and his work is his
    A. dependability
    B. quantity of work done
    C. quality of work done
    D. education and training

    12.____

13. When a District Superintendent first assumes his command, it is LEAST important for him at the beginning to observe
    A. how his equipment is designed and its adaptability
    B. how to reorganize the district for greater efficiency
    C. the capabilities of the men in the district
    D. the methods of operation being employed

    13.____

14. When making an inspection of one of the buildings under your supervision, the BEST procedure to follow in making a record of the inspection is to
    A. return immediately to the office and write a report from memory
    B. write down all the important facts during or as soon as you complete the inspection
    C. fix in your mind all important facts so that you can repeat them from memory if necessary
    D. fix in your mind all important facts so that you can make out your report at the end of the day

15. Assume that your superior has directed you to make certain changes in your established procedure. After using this modified procedure on several occasions, you find that the original procedure was distinctly superior and you wish to return to it.
You should
    A. let your superior find this out for himself
    B. simply change back to the original procedure
    C. compile definite data and information to prove your case to your superior
    D. persuade one of the more experienced workers to take this matter up with your superior

16. An inspector visited a large building under construction. He inspected the soil lines at 9 A.M., water lines at 10 A.M., fixtures at 11 A.M., and did his office work in the afternoon. He followed the same pattern daily for weeks.
This procedure was
    A. *good*, because it was methodical and he did not miss anything
    B. *good*, because it gave equal time to all phases of the plumbing
    C. *bad*, because not enough time was devoted to fixtures
    D. *bad*, because the tradesmen knew when the inspection would occur

17. Assume that one of the foremen in a training course, which you are conducting, proposes a poor solution for a maintenance problem.
Of the following, the BEST course of action for you to take is to
    A. accept the solution tentatively and correct it during the next class meeting
    B. point out all the defects of this proposed solution and wait until somebody thinks of a better solution
    C. try to get the class to reject this proposed solution and develop a better solution
    D. let the matter pass since somebody will present a better solution as the class work proceeds

18. As a supervisor, you should be seeking ways to improve the efficiency of shop operations by means such as changing established work procedures.
The following are offered as possible actions that you should consider in changing established work procedures:
    I. Make changes only when your foremen agree to them
    II. Discuss changes with your supervisor before putting them into practice

III. Standardize any operation which is performed on a continuing basis
IV. Make changes quickly and quietly in order to avoid dissent
V. Secure expert guidance before instituting unfamiliar procedures
Of the following suggested answers, the one that describes the actions to be taken to change established work procedures is
   A. I, IV, V   B. II, III, V   C. III, IV, V   D. All of the above

19. A supervisor determined that a foreman, without informing his superior, delegated responsibility for checking time cards to a member of his gang. The supervisor then called the foreman into his office where he reprimanded the foreman.
This action of the supervisor in reprimanding the foreman was
   A. *proper*, because the checking of time cards is the foreman's responsibility and should not be delegated
   B. *proper*, because the foreman did not ask the supervisor for permission to delegate responsibility
   C. *improper*, because the foreman may no longer take the initiative in solving future problems
   D. *improper*, because the supervisor is interfering in a function which is not his responsibility

20. A capable supervisor should check all operations under his control.
Of the following, the LEAST important reason for doing this is to make sure that
   A. operations are being performed as scheduled
   B. he personally observes all operations at all times
   C. all the operations are still needed
   D. his manpower is being utilized efficiently

21. A supervisor makes it a practice to apply fair and firm discipline in all cases of rule infractions, including those of a minor nature.
This practice should PRIMARILY be considered
   A. *bad*, since applying discipline for minor violations is a waste of time
   B. *good*, because not applying discipline for minor infractions can lead to a more serious erosion of discipline
   C. *bad*, because employees do not like to be disciplined for minor violations of the rules
   D. *good*, because violating any rule can cause a dangerous situation to occur

22. A maintainer would PROPERLY consider it poor supervisory practice for a foreman to consult with him on
   A. which of several repair jobs should be scheduled first
   B. how to cope with personal problems at home
   C. whether the neatness of his headquarters can be improved
   D. how to express a suggestion which the maintainer plans to submit formally

23. Assume that you have determined that the work of one of your foremen and the men he supervises is consistently behind schedule. When you discuss this situation with the foreman, he tells you that his men are poor workers and then complains that he must spend all of his time checking on their work.
The following actions are offered for your consideration as possible ways of solving the problem of poor performance of the foreman and his men:
   I. Review the work standards with the foreman and determine whether they are realistic.
   II. Tell the foreman that you will recommend him for the foreman's training course for retraining.
   III. Ask the foreman for the names of the maintainers and then replace them as soon as possible.
   IV. Tell the foreman that you expect him to meet a satisfactory level of performance.
   V. Tell the foreman to insist that his men work overtime to catch up to the schedule.
   VI. Tell the foreman to review the type and amount of training he has given the maintainers.
   VII. Tell the foreman that he will be out of a job if he does not produce on schedule.
   VIII. Avoid all criticism of the foreman and his methods.
   Which of the following suggested answers CORRECTLY lists the proper actions to be taken to solve the problem of poor performance of the foreman and his men?
   A. I, II, IV, VI   B. I, III, V, VII   C. II, III, VI, VIII   D. IV, V, VI, VIII

23._____

24. When a conference or a group discussion is tending to turn into a *bull session* without constructive purpose, the BEST action to take is to
   A. reprimand the leader of the bull session
   B. redirect the discussion to the business at hand
   C. dismiss the meeting and reschedule it for another day
   D. allow the bull session to continue

24._____

25. Assume that you have been assigned responsibility for a program in which a high production rate is mandatory. From past experience, you know that your foremen do not perform equally well in the various types of jobs given to them. Which of the following methods should you use in selecting foremen for the specific types of work involved in the program?
   A. Leave the method of selecting foremen to your supervisor
   B. Assign each foreman to the work he does best
   C. Allow each foreman to choose his own job
   D. Assign each foreman to a job which will permit him to improve his own abilities

25._____

KEY (CORRECT ANSWERS)

1.	B	11.	C
2.	B	12.	D
3.	A	13.	B
4.	D	14.	B
5.	D	15.	C
6.	B	16.	D
7.	B	17.	C
8.	B	18.	B
9.	A	19.	A
10.	D	20.	B

21.	B
22.	A
23.	A
24.	B
25.	B

TEST 2

DIRECTIONS: Each question or incomplete statement is followed by several suggested answers or completions. Select the one that BEST answers the question or completes the statement. *PRINT THE LETTER OF THE CORRECT ANSWER IN THE SPACE AT THE RIGHT.*

1. A foreman who is familiar with modern management principles should know that the one of the following requirements of an administrator which is LEAST important is his ability to
   A. coordinate work
   B. plan, organize, and direct the work under his control
   C. cooperate with others
   D. perform the duties of the employees under his jurisdiction

2. When subordinates request his advice in solving problems encountered in their work, a certain chief occasionally answers the request by first asking the subordinate what he thinks should be done.
   This action by the chief is, on the whole,
   A. *desirable*, because it stimulates subordinates to give more thought to the solution of problems encountered
   B. *undesirable*, because it discourages subordinates from asking questions
   C. *desirable*, because it discourages subordinates from asking questions
   D. *undesirable*, because it undermines the confidence of subordinates in the ability of their supervisor

3. Of the following factors that may be considered by a unit head in dealing with the tardy subordinate, the one which should be given LEAST consideration is the
   A. frequency with which the employee is tardy
   B. effect of the employee's tardiness upon the work of other employees
   C. willingness of the employee to work overtime when necessary
   D. cause of the employee's tardiness

4. The MOST important requirement of a good inspectional report is that it should be
   A. properly addressed   B. lengthy
   C. clear and brief   D. spelled correctly

5. Building superintendents frequently inquire about departmental inspectional procedures.
   Of the following, it is BEST to
   A. advise them to write to the department for an official reply
   B. refuse as the inspectional procedure is a restricted matter
   C. briefly explain the procedure to them
   D. avoid the inquiry by changing the subject

6. Reprimanding a crew member before other workers is a
    A. *good* practice; the reprimand serves as a warning to the other workers
    B. *bad* practice; people usually resent criticism made in public
    C. *good* practice; the other workers will realize that the supervisor is fair
    D. *bad* practice; the other workers will take sides in the dispute

7. Of the following actions, the one which is LEAST likely to promote good work is for the group leader to
    A. praise workers for doing a good job
    B. call attention to the opportunities for promotion for better workers
    C. threaten to recommend discharge of workers who are below standard
    D. put into practice any good suggestion made by crew members

8. A supervisor notices that a member of his crew has skipped a routine step in his job.
    Of the following, the BEST action for the supervisor to take is to
    A. promptly question the worker about the incident
    B. immediately assign another man to complete the job
    C. bring up the incident the next time the worker asks for a favor
    D. say nothing about the incident but watch the worker carefully in the future

9. Assume you have been told to show a new worker how to operate a piece of equipment.
    Your FIRST step should be to
    A. ask the worker if he has any questions about the equipment
    B. permit the worker to operate the equipment himself while you carefully watch to prevent damage
    C. demonstrate the operation of the equipment for the worker
    D. have the worker read an instruction booklet on the maintenance of the equipment

10. Whenever a new man was assigned to his crew, the supervisor would introduce him to all other crew members, take him on a tour of the plant, tell him about bus schedules and places to eat.
    This practice is
    A. *good*; the new man is made to feel welcome
    B. *bad*; supervisors should not interfere in personal matters
    C. *good*; the new man knows that he can bring his personal problems to the supervisor
    D. *bad*; work time should not be spent on personal matters

11. The MOST important factor in successful leadership is the ability to
    A. obtain instant obedience to all orders
    B. establish friendly personal relations with crew members
    C. avoid disciplining crew members
    D. make crew members want to do what should be done

12. Explaining the reasons for departmental procedure to workers tends to
    A. waste time which should be used for productive purposes
    B. increase their interest in their work
    C. make them more critical of departmental procedures
    D. confuse them

13. If you want a job done well do it yourself.
    For a supervisor to follow this advice would be
    A. *good*; a supervisor is responsible for the work of his crew
    B. *bad*; a supervisor should train his men, not do their work
    C. *good*; a supervisor should be skilled in all jobs assigned to his crew
    D. *bad*; a supervisor loses respect when he works with his hands

14. When a supervisor discovers a mistake in one of the jobs for which his crew is responsible, it is MOST important for him to find out
    A. whether anybody else knows about the mistake
    B. who was to blame for the mistake
    C. how to prevent similar mistakes in the future
    D. whether similar mistakes occurred in the past

15. A supervisor who has to explain a new procedure to his crew should realize that questions from the crew USUALLY show that they
    A. are opposed to the new practice
    B. are completely confused by the explanation
    C. need more training in the new procedure
    D. are interested in the explanation

16. A good way for a supervisor to retain the confidence of his or her employees is to
    A. say as little as possible
    B. check work frequently
    C. make no promises unless they will be fulfilled
    D. never hesitate in giving an answer to any question

17. Good supervision is ESSENTIALLY a matter of
    A. patience in supervising workers   B. care in selecting workers
    C. skill in human relations   D. fairness in disciplining workers

18. It is MOST important for an employee who has been assigned a monotonous task to
    A. perform this task before doing other work
    B. ask another employee to help
    C. perform this task only after all other work has been completed
    D. take measures to prevent mistakes in performing the task

4 (#2)

19. One of your employees has violated a minor agency regulation.
The FIRST thing you should do is
    A. warn the employee that you will have to take disciplinary action if it should happen again
    B. ask the employee to explain his or her actions
    C. inform your supervisor and wait for advice
    D. write a memo describing the incident and place it in the employee's personnel file

19._____

20. One of your employees tells you that he feels you give him much more work than the other employees, and he is having trouble meeting your deadlines.
You should
    A. ask if he has been under a lot of non-work related stress lately
    B. review his recent assignments to determine if he is correct
    C. explain that this is a busy time, but you are dividing the work equally
    D. tell him that he is the most competent employee and that is why he receives more work

20._____

21. A supervisor assigns one of his crew to complete a portion of a job. A short time later, the supervisor notices that the portion has not been completed.
Of the following, the BEST way for the supervisor to handle this is to
    A. ask the crew member why he has not completed the assignment
    B. reprimand the crew member for not obeying orders
    C. assign another crew member to complete the assignment
    D. complete the assignment himself

21._____

22. Supposes that a member of your crew complains that you are *playing favorites* in assigning work.
Of the following, the BEST method of handling the complaint is to
    A. deny it and refuse to discuss the matter with the worker
    B. take the opportunity to tell the worker what is wrong with his work
    C. ask the worker for examples to prove his point and try to clear up any misunderstanding
    D. promise to be more careful in making assignments in the future

22._____

23. A member of your crew comes to you with a complaint. After discussing the matter with him, it is clear that you have convinced him that his complaint was not justified.
At this point, you should
    A. permit him to drop the matter
    B. make him admit his error
    C. pretend to see some justification in his complaint
    D. warn him against making unjustified complaints

23._____

24. Suppose that a supervisor has in his crew an older man who works rather slowly. In other respects, this man is a good worker; he is seldom absent, works carefully, never loafs, and is cooperative.

24._____

The BEST way for the supervisor to handle this worker is to
   A. try to get him to work faster and less carefully
   B. give him the most disagreeable job
   C. request that he be given special training
   D. permit him to work at his own speed

25. Suppose that a member of your crew comes to you with a suggestion he thinks will save time in doing a job. You realize immediately that it won't work. Under these circumstances, your BEST action would be to
   A. thank the worker for the suggestion and forget about it
   B. explain to the worker why you think it won't work
   C. tell the worker to put the suggestion in writing
   D. ask the other members of your crew to criticize the suggestion

25.____

KEY (CORRECT ANSWERS)

1. D
2. A
3. C
4. C
5. C

6. B
7. C
8. A
9. C
10. A

11. D
12. B
13. B
14. C
15. D

16. C
17. C
18. D
19. B
20. B

21. A
22. C
23. A
24. D
25. B

EXAMINATION SECTION
TEST 1

DIRECTIONS: Each question or incomplete statement is followed by several suggested answers or completions. Select the one that BEST answers the question or completes the statement. *PRINT THE LETTER OF THE CORRECT ANSWER IN THE SPACE AT THE RIGHT.*

1. A *basic* method of operation that a *good* supervisor should follow is to

    A. check the work of subordinates constantly to make sure they are not making exceptions to the rules
    B. train subordinates so they can handle problems that come up regularly themselves and come to him only with special cases
    C. delegate to subordinates only those duties which he cannot do himself
    D. issue directions to subordinates only on special matters

    1.____

2. To do a *good* job of performance evaluation, it is BEST for a supervisor to

    A. compare the employee's performance to that of another employee doing similar work
    B. give greatest weight to instances of unusually good or unusually poor performance
    C. leave out any consideration of the employee's personal traits
    D. measure the employee's performance against standard performance requirements

    2.____

3. Of the following, the MOST important reason for a supervisor to have private face to face discussions with subordinates about their performance is to

    A. help employees improve their work
    B. give special praise to employees who perform well
    C. encourage the employees to compete for higher performance ratings
    D. discipline employees who perform poorly

    3.____

4. Of the following, the CHIEF purpose of a probationary period for a new employee is to allow time for

    A. finding out whether the selection processes are satisfactory
    B. the employee to make adjustments in his home circumstances made necessary by the job
    C. the employee to decide whether he wants a permanent appointment
    D. determining the fitness of the employee to continue in the job

    4.____

5. When a subordinate resigns his job, it is MOST important to conduct an exit interview in order to

    A. try to get the employee to remain on the job
    B. learn the true reasons for the employee's resignation
    C. see that the employee leaves with a good opinion of the agency
    D. ask the employee if he would consider a transfer

    5.____

6. Chronic lateness of employees is generally LEAST likely to be due to

    A. distance of job location from home
    B. poor personnel administration
    C. unexpressed employee grievances
    D. low morale

    6.____

107

7. Of the following, the LEAST effective stimulus for motivating employees toward improved performance over a long-range period is

   A. their sense of achievement
   B. their feeling of recognition
   C. opportunity for their self-development
   D. an increase in salary

8. Suppose that NOT ONE of a group of employees has turned in an idea to the employees suggestion system during the past year.
   The *most probable* reason for this situation is that the

   A. money awards given for suggestions used are not high enough to make employees interested
   B. employees in this group are not able to develop any good ideas
   C. supervisor of these employees is not doing enough to encourage them to take part in the program
   D. methods and procedures of operation do not need improvement

9. A subordinate tells you that he is having trouble concentrating on his work due to a personal problem at home.
   Of the following, it would be BEST for you to

   A. refer him to a community service agency
   B. listen quietly to the story because he may just need a sympathetic ear
   C. tell him that you cannot help him because the problem is not job related
   D. ask him questions about the nature of the problem and tell him how you would handle it

10. For you as a supervisor to give each of your subordinates *exactly* the same type of supervision is

    A. *advisable*, because doing this insures fair and impartial treatment of each individual
    B. *not advisable*, because individuals like to think that they are receiving better treatment than others
    C. *advisable*, because once a supervisor learns how to deal with a subordinate who brings a problem to him, he can handle another subordinate with this problem in the same way
    D. *not advisable*, because each person is different and there is no one supervisory procedure for dealing with individuals that applies in every case

11. A senior employee under your supervision tells you that he is reluctant to speak to one of his subordinates about his poor work habits, because this worker is "strong-willed" and he does not want to antagonize him.
    For you to offer to speak to the subordinate about this matter yourself would be

    A. *advisable*, since you are in a position of greater authority
    B. *inadvisable*, since handling this problem is a basic supervisory responsibility of the senior employee
    C. *advisable*, since the senior employee must work more closely with the worker than you do
    D. *inadvisable*, since you should not risk antagonizing the employee yourself

12. Some of your subordinates have been coming to you with complaints you feel are unimportant. For you to hear their stories out is

    A. *poor practice,* you should spend your time on more important matters
    B. *good practice,* this will increase your popularity with your subordinates
    C. *poor practice,* subordinates should learn to come to you only with major grievances
    D. *good practice,* it may prevent minor complaints from developing into major grievances

13. Assume that an agency has an established procedure for handling employee grievances. An employee in this agency, comes to his immediate supervisor with a grievance. The supervisor investigates the matter and makes a decision.
    However, the employee is not satisfied with the decision made by the supervisor. The BEST action for the supervisor to take is to

    A. tell the employee he will review the matter further
    B. remind the employee that he is the supervisor and the employee must act in accordance with his decision
    C. explain to the employee how he can carry his complaint forward to the next step in the grievance procedure
    D. tell the employee he will consult with his own superiors on the matter

14. Subordinate employees and senior employees often must make quick decisions while in the field. The supervisor can BEST help subordinates meet such situations by

    A. training them in the appropriate action to take for every problem that may come up
    B. limiting the areas in which they are permitted to make decisions
    C. making certain they understand clearly the basic policies of the bureau and the department
    D. delegating authority to make such decisions to only a few subordinates on each level

15. Studies have shown that the CHIEF cause of failure to achieve success as a supervisor is

    A. an unwillingness to delegate authority to subordinates
    B. the establishment of high performance standards for subordinates
    C. the use of discipline that is too strict
    D. showing too much leniency to poor workers

16. When a supervisor delegates to a subordinate certain work that he normally does himself, it is MOST important that he give the subordinate

    A. responsibility for also setting the standards for the work to be done
    B. sufficient authority to be able to carry out the assignment
    C. written, step-by-step instructions for doing the work
    D. an explanation of one part of the task at a time

17. It is particularly important that disciplinary actions be equitable as between individuals. This statement *implies* that

    A. punishment applied in disciplinary actions should be lenient
    B. proposed disciplinary actions should be reviewed by higher authority
    C. subordinates should have an opportunity to present their stories before penalties are applied
    D. penalties for violations of the rules should be standardized and consistently applied

18. You discover that from time to time a number of false rumors circulate among your subordinates.
    Of the following, the BEST way for you to handle this situation is to

    A. ignore the rumors since rumors circulate in every office and can never be eliminated
    B. attempt to find those responsible for the rumors and reprimand them
    C. make sure that your employees are informed as soon as possible about all matters that affect them
    D. inform your superior about the rumors and let him deal with the matter

19. Supervisors who allow the "halo effect" to influence their evaluations of subordinates are *most likely* to

    A. give more lenient ratings to older employees who have longer service
    B. let one highly favorable or unfavorable trait unduly affect their judgment of an employee
    C. evaluate all employees on one trait before considering a second
    D. give high evaluations in order to avoid antagonizing their subordinates

20. For a supervisor to keep records of reprimands to subordinates about infractions of the rules is

    A. *good practice,* because these records are valuable to support disciplinary actions recommended or taken
    B. *poor practice,* because such records are evidence of the supervisor's inability to maintain discipline
    C. *good practice,* because such records indicate that the supervisor is doing a good job
    D. *poor practice,* because the best way to correct subordinates is to give them more training

21. When a new departmental policy has been established, it would be MOST advisable for you, as a supervisor, to

    A. distribute a memo which states the new policy and instruct your subordinates to read it
    B. explain specifically to your subordinates how the policy is going to affect them
    C. make sure your subordinates understand that you are not responsible for setting the policy
    D. tell your subordinates whether you agree or disagree with the policy

22. As a supervisor, you receive several complaints about the rude conduct of a subordinate. The FIRST action you should take is to

    A. request his transfer to another office
    B. prepare a charge sheet for disciplinary action
    C. assign a senior employee to work with him for a week
    D. interview the employee to determine possible reason, and warn that correction is necessary

23. A supervisor is *most likely* to get subordinates to work cooperatively toward accomplishing bureau goals if he

    A. creates an atmosphere that contributes to their feeling of security
    B. backs up subordinates even when they occasionally disobey regulations
    C. shows interest in subordinates by helping them solve their personal problems
    D. uses an authoritarian or "bossy" approach to supervision

24. A supervisor is holding a staff meeting with his senior employees to try to find an acceptable solution to a problem that has come up.
    Of the following, the CHIEF role of the supervisor at this meeting should be to

    A. see that every member of the group contributes at least one suggestions
    B. act as chairman of the meeting, but take no other active part to avoid influencing the senior employees
    C. keep the participants from wandering off into discussions of irrelevant matters
    D. make certain the participants hear his views on the matter at the beginning of the meeting

25. An employee shows you a certificate that he has just received for completing two years of study in conversational Spanish. As his supervisor, it would be BEST for you to

    A. put a note about this accomplishment in his personnel folder
    B. assign him to areas in which people of Spanish origin live
    C. congratulate him on this accomplishment, but tell him frankly that you doubt this is likely to have any direct bearing on his work
    D. encourage him to continue his studies and become thoroughly fluent in speaking the language

KEY (CORRECT ANSWERS)

1. B
2. D
3. A
4. D
5. B

6. A
7. D
8. C
9. B
10. D

11. B
12. D
13. C
14. C
15. A

16. B
17. D
18. C
19. B
20. A

21. B
22. D
23. A
24. C
25. A

TEST 2

DIRECTIONS: Each question or incomplete statement is followed by several suggested answers or completions. Select the one that BEST answers the question or completes the statement. *PRINT THE LETTER OF THE CORRECT ANSWER IN THE SPACE AT THE RIGHT.*

1. Of the following, the factor affecting employee morale which the immediate supervisor is LEAST able to control is

    A. handling of grievances
    B. fair and impartial treatment of subordinates
    C. general presonnel rules and regulations
    D. accident prevention

2. When one of your workers does outstanding work, you should

    A. explain to your other employees that you expect the same kind of work of them
    B. praise him for his work so that he will know it is appreciated
    C. say nothing, because other employees may think you are showing favoritism
    D. show him how his work can be improved still more so that he will not sit back

3. For you as a supervisor to consider a suggestion from a probationary worker for improving a procedure would be

    A. *poor practice,* because this employee is too new on the job to know much about it
    B. *good practice,* because you may be able to share credit for the suggestion
    C. *poor practice,* because it may hurt the morale of the older employees
    D. *good practice,* because the suggestion may be worthwhile

4. If you find you must criticize the work of one of your workers, it would be BEST for you to

    A. mention the good points in his work as well as the faults
    B. caution him that he will receive an unsatisfactory performance report unless his work improves
    C. compare his work to that of the other agents you supervise
    D. apologize for making the criticism

5. As a senior employee which one of the following matters would it be BEST for you to talk over with your supervisor before you take final action?

    A. One of the workers you supervise continues to disregard your instructions repeatedly in spite of repeated warnings
    B. One of your workers tells you he wants to discuss a personal problem
    C. A probationary employee tells you he does not understand a procedure
    D. One of your workers tells you he disagrees with the way you rate his work

6. If one of your subordinates asks you a question about a department rule and you do not know the answer, you should tell him that

    A. he should try to get the information himself
    B. you do not have the answer, but you will get it for him as soon as you can
    C. he should ask you the question again a week from now
    D. he should put the question in writing

7. If, as a supervisor, you realize that you have been unfair in criticizing one of your subordinates, the BEST action for you to take is to

   A. say nothing, but overlook some error made by this employee in the future
   B. be frank and tell the employee that you are sorry for the mistake you made
   C. let the employee know in some indirect way without admitting your mistake, that you realize he was not at fault
   D. say nothing, but be more careful about criticizing subordinates in the future

8. Of the following, the MOST important reason for a supervisor to write an accident report as soon as possible after an accident has happened is to

   A. make sure that important facts about the accident are not forgotten
   B. avoid delay in getting compensation for the injured person
   C. get adequate medical treatment for the injured person
   D. keep department accident statistics up to date

9. In any matter which may require disciplinary action, the FIRST responsibility of the supervisor is to

   A. decide what penalty should be applied for the offense
   B. refer the matter to a higher authority for complete investigation
   C. place the interests of the department above those of the employee
   D. investigate the matter fully to get all the facts

10. Suppose you find it necessary to criticize one of the subordinates you supervise. You should

    A. send an official letter to his home
    B. speak to him about the matter privately
    C. speak to him at a staff meeting
    D. ask another worker who is friendly with him to talk to him about the matter

11. Some of your subordinates have been coming to you with complaints you feel are unimportant. For you to hear their stories out is

    A. *poor practice,* you should spend your time on more important matters
    B. *good practice,* this will increase your popularity with your subordinates
    C. *poor practice,* subordinates should learn to come to you only with major grievances
    D. *good practice,* it may prevent minor complaints from developing into major grievances

12. Suppose that NOT ONE of a group of employees has turned in an idea to the employees' suggestion system during the past year. The *most probable* reason for this situation is that the

    A. supervisor of these employees is not doing enough to encourage them to take part in this program
    B. employees in this group are not able to develop any good ideas
    C. money awards given for suggestions used are not high enough to make employees interested
    D. methods and procedures of operation do not need improvement

13. For you as a supervisor to give each of your subordinates *exactly* the same type of supervision is

    A. *advisable,* because doing this insures fair and impartial treatment of each individual
    B. *not advisable,* because each person is different and there is no one supervisory procedure for dealing with individuals that applies in every case
    C. *advisable,* because once a supervisor learns how to deal with a subordinate who brings a problem to him, he can handle another subordinate with this problem in the same way
    D. *not advisable,* because individuals like to think that they are receiving better treatment than others

14. In evaluating personnel, a supervisor should keep in mind that the MOST important objective of performance evaluations is to

    A. encourage employees to compete for higher performance ratings
    B. give recognition to employees who perform well
    C. help employees improve their work
    D. discipline employees who perform poorly

15. A subordinate tells you that he is having trouble concentrating on his work due to a personal problem at home. Of the following, it would be BEST for you to

    A. refer him to a community service agency
    B. listen quietly to the story because he may just need a sympathetic ear
    C. tell him that you cannot help him because the problem is not job-related
    D. ask him some questions about the nature of the problem and tell him how you would handle it

16. To do a good job of performance evaluation, it is BEST for a supervisor to

    A. measure the employee's performance against standard performance requirements
    B. compare the employee's performance to that of another employee doing similar work
    C. leave out any consideration of the employee's personal traits
    D. give greatest weight to instances of unusually good or unusually poor performance

17. It is particularly important that disciplinary actions be equitable as between individuals. This statement *implies* that

    A. punishment applied in disciplinary actions should be lenient
    B. proposed disciplinary actions should be reviewed by higher authority
    C. subordinates should have an opportunity to present their stories before penalties are applied
    D. penalties for violations of the rules should be standardized and consistently applied

18. Assume that an agency has an established procedure for handling employee grievances. An employee in this agency comes to his immediate supervisor with a grievance. The supervisor investigates the matter and makes a decision. However, the employee is not satisfied with the decision made by the supervisor.
    The BEST action for the supervisor to take is to

A. tell the employee he will review the matter further
B. remind the employee that he is the supervisor and the employee must act in accordance with his decision
C. explain to the employee how he can carry his complaint forward to the next step in the grievance procedure
D. tell the employee he will consult with his own superiors on the matter

19. Of the following, the CHIEF purpose of a probationary period for a new employee is to allow time for 19.____

    A. finding out whether the selection processes are satisfactory
    B. determining the fitness of the employee to continue in the job
    C. the employee to decide whether he wants a permanent appointment
    D. the employee to make adjustments in his home circumstances made necessary by the job

20. Of the following, the subject that would be MOST important to include in a "break-in" program for new employees is 20.____

    A. explanation of rules, regulations and policies of the agency
    B. Instruction in the agency's history and programs
    C. explanation of the importance of the new employees' own particular job
    D. explanation of the duties and responsibilities of the employee

21. Suppose a new employee under your supervision seems slow to learn and is making mistakes in performing his duties. Your FIRST action should be to 21.____

    A. pass this information on to the bureau director
    B. reprimand the worker so he will not repeat these mistakes
    C. find out whether this worker understands your instructions
    D. note these facts for future reference when writing up the monthly performance evaluation

22. In training new employees to do a certain job it would be LEAST desirable for you to 22.____

    A. demonstrate how the job is done, step by step
    B. encourage the workers to ask questions if they aren't clear about any point
    C. tell them about the various mistakes other agents have made in doing this job
    D. have the workers do the job, explaining to you what they are doing and why

23. One of the workers under your supervision is resentful when you ask her to remove her jangling bracelets before she starts her tour of duty. 23.____
    Of the following, the BEST explanation you can give her for the rule against wearing such jewelry while on duty is that

    A. the jewelry may create a safety hazard
    B. employees must give up certain personal liberties if they want to keep their jobs
    C. workers cannot perform their duties as efficiently if they wear distracting jewelry
    D. citizens may receive an unfavorable impression of the department

24. Of the following, the LEAST important reason for having a department handbook and a bureau standard operating procedure is to

 A. help in training new employees
 B. provide a source of reference for department and bureau rules and procedures
 C. prevent errors in work by providing clear guidelines
 D. make the supervisor's job easy

25. On inspecting your squad prior to their tour of duty, you note an employee improperly and unacceptably dressed.
The FIRST action you should take is to

 A. call the employee aside and insist on immediate correction if possible
 B. notify the district commander right away
 C. have the employee submit a memorandum explaining the reason for the improper uniform
 D. permit the employee to proceed on duty but warn him not to let this happen again

KEY (CORRECT ANSWERS)

1.	C	11.	D
2.	B	12.	A
3.	D	13.	B
4.	A	14.	C
5.	A	15.	B
6.	B	16.	A
7.	B	17.	D
8.	A	18.	C
9.	D	19.	B
10.	B	20.	D

21.	C
22.	C
23.	D
24.	D
25.	A

WORK SCHEDULING

EXAMINATION SECTION
TEST 1

DIRECTIONS: Each question or incomplete statement is followed by several suggested answers or completions. Select the one that BEST answers the question or completes the statement. *PRINT THE LETTER OF THE CORRECT ANSWER IN THE SPACE AT THE RIGHT.*

Questions 1-6.

DIRECTIONS: Questions 1 through 6 are to be answered SOLELY on the basis of the information given in the ELEVATOR OPERATORS' WORK SCHEDULE shown below.

ELEVATOR OPERATORS' WORK SCHEDULE				
Operator	Hours of Work	A.M. Relief Period	Lunch Hour	P.M. Relief Period
Anderson	8:30-4:30	10:20-10:30	12:00-1:00	2:20-2:30
Carter	8:00-4:00	10:10-10:20	11:45-12:45	2:30-2:40
Daniels	9:00-5:00	10:20-10:30	12:30-1:30	3:15-3:25
Grand	9:30-5:30	11:30-11:40	1:00-2:00	4:05-4:15
Jones	7:45-3:45	9:45-9:55	11:30-12:30	2:05-2:15
Lewis	9:45-5:45	11:40-11:50	1:15-2:15	4:20-4:30
Nance	8:45-4:45	10:50-11:00	12:30-1:30	3:05-3:15
Perkins	8:00-4:00	10:00-10:10	12:00-1:00	2:40-2:50
Russo	7:45-3:45	9:30-9:40	11:30-12:30	2:10-2:20
Smith	9:45-5:45	11:45-11:55	1:15-2:15	4:05-4:15

1. The two operators who are on P.M. relief at the SAME time are

   A. Anderson and Daniels B. Carter and Perkins
   C. Jones and Russo D. Grand and Smith

   1.____

2. Of the following, the two operators who have the SAME lunch hour are

   A. Anderson and Perkins B. Daniels and Russo
   C. Grand and Smith D. Nance and Russo

   2.____

3. At 12:15, the number of operators on their lunch hour is

   A. 3 B. 4 C. 5 D. 6

   3.____

4. The operator who has an A.M. relief period right after Perkins and a P.M. relief period right before Perkins is

   A. Russo B. Nance C. Daniels D. Carter

   4.____

5. The number of operators who are scheduled to be working at 4:40 is

   A. 5 B. 6 C. 7 D. 8

   5.____

6. According to the schedule, it is MOST correct to say that 6.____
   A. no operator has a relief period during the time that another operator has a lunch hour
   B. each operator has to wait an identical amount of time between the end of lunch and the beginning of P.M. relief period
   C. no operator has a relief period before 9:45 or after 4:00
   D. each operator is allowed a total of 1 hour and 20 minutes for lunch hour and relief periods

---

KEY (CORRECT ANSWERS)

1. D
2. A
3. C
4. D
5. A
6. D

TEST 2

DIRECTIONS: Each question or incomplete statement is followed by several suggested answers or completions. Select the one that BEST answers the question or completes the statement. *PRINT THE LETTER OF THE CORRECT ANSWER IN THE SPACE AT THE RIGHT.*

Questions 1-7.

DIRECTIONS: Questions 1 through 7 are to be answered SOLELY on the basis of the time sheet and instructions given below.

The following time sheet indicates the times that seven laundry workers arrived and left each day for the week of August 23. The times they arrived for work are shown under the heading IN, and the times they left are shown under the heading OUT. The letter (P) indicates time which was used for personal business. Time used for this purpose is charged to annual leave. Lunch time is one-half hour from noon to 12:30 P.M. and is not accounted for on this time record.

The employees on this shift are scheduled to work from 8:00 A.M. to 4:00 P.M. Lateness is charged to annual leave. Reporting after 8:00 A.M. is considered late.

	MON.		TUES.		WED.		THURS.		FRI.	
	AM IN	PM OUT	AM IN	PM OUT	AM IN	PM OUT	AM IN	PM OUT	AM IN	PM OUT
Baxter	7:50	4:01	7:49	4:07	8:00	4:07	8:20	4:00	7:42	4:03
Gardner	8:02	4:00	8:20	4:00	8:05	3:30(P)	8:00	4:03	8:00	4:07
Clements	8:00	4:04	8:03	4:01	7:59	4:00	7:54	4:06	7:59	4:00
Tompkins	7:56	4:00	Annual leave		8:00	4:07	7:59	4:00	8:00	4:01
Wagner	8:04	4:03	7:40	4:00	7:53	4:04	8:00	4:09	7:53	4:00
Patterson	8:00	2:30(P)	8:15	4:04	Sick leave		7:45	4:00	7:59	4:04
Cunningham	7:43	4:02	7:50	4:00	7:59	4:02	8:00	4:10	8:00	4:00

1. Which one of the following laundry workers did NOT have any time charged to annual leave or sick leave during the week?   1.____

   A. Gardner   B. Clements   C. Tompkins   D. Cunningham

2. On which day did ALL the laundry workers arrive on time?   2.____

   A. Monday   B. Wednesday   C. Thursday   D. Friday

3. Which of the following laundry workers used time to take care of personal business?   3.____

   A. Baxter and Clements
   C. Gardner and Patterson
   B. Patterson and Cunningham
   D. Wagner and Tompkins

4. How many laundry workers were late on Monday?   4.____

   A. 1   B. 2   C. 3   D. 4

5. Which one of the following laundry workers arrived late on three of the five days?   5.____

   A. Baxter   B. Gardner   C. Wagner   D. Patterson

121

6. The percentage of laundry workers reporting to work late on Tuesday is MOST NEARLY 6._____
   A. 15%   B. 25%   C. 45%   D. 50%

7. The percentage of laundry workers that were absent for an entire day during the week is MOST NEARLY 7._____
   A. 6%   B. 9%   C. 15%   D. 30%

KEY (CORRECT ANSWERS)

1. D
2. D
3. C
4. B
5. B
6. C
7. D

TEST 3

Questions 1-9.

DIRECTIONS: Questions 1 through 9 are to be answered SOLELY on the basis of the following information and timesheet given below.

The following is a foreman's timesheet for his crew for one week. The hours worked each day or the reason the man was off on that day are shown on the sheet. *R* means rest day. *A* means annual leave. *S* means sick leave. Where a man worked only part of a day, both the number of hours worked and the number of hours taken off are entered. The reason for absence is entered in parentheses next to the number of hours taken off.

Name	Saturday	Sunday	Monday	Tuesday	Wednesday	Thursday	Friday
Smith	R	R	7	7	7	3 4(A)	7
Jones	R	7	7	7	7	7	R
Green	R	R	7	7	S	S	S
White	R	R	7	7	A	7	7
Doe	7	7	7	7	7	R	R
Brown	R	R	A	7	7	7	7
Black	R	R	S	7	7	7	7
Reed	R	R	7	7	7	7	S
Roe	R	R	A	7	7	7	7
Lane	7	R	R	7	7	A	S

1. The caretaker who worked EXACTLY 21 hours during the week is

    A. Lane   B. Roe   C. Smith   D. White

2. The TOTAL number of hours worked by all caretakers during the week is

    A. 268   B. 276   C. 280   D. 288

3. The two days of the week on which MOST caretakers were off are

    A. Thursday and Friday   B. Friday and Saturday
    C. Saturday and Sunday   D. Sunday and Monday

4. The day on which three caretakers were off on sick leave is

    A. Monday   B. Friday   C. Saturday   D. Sunday

5. The two workers who took LEAST time off during the week are

    A. Doe and Reed   B. Jones and Doe
    C. Reed and Smith   D. Smith and Jones

6. The caretaker who worked the LEAST number of hours during the week is

    A. Brown   B. Green   C. Lane   D. Roe

7. The caretakers who did NOT work on Thursday are

    A. Doe, White, and Smith
    B. Green, Doe, and Lane
    C. Green, Doe, and Smith
    D. Green, Lane, and Smith

123

8. The day on which one caretaker worked ONLY 3 hours is   8._____
   A. Friday   B. Saturday   C. Thursday   D. Wednesday

9. The day on which ALL caretakers worked is   9._____
   A. Monday   B. Thursday   C. Tuesday   D. Wednesday

KEY (CORRECT ANSWERS)

1. A
2. B
3. C
4. B
5. B

6. B
7. B
8. C
9. C

TEST 4

Questions 1-6.

DIRECTIONS: Questions 1 through 6 are to be answered SOLELY on the basis of the table below which shows the initial requests made by staff for vacation. It is to be used with the RULES AND GUIDELINES to make the decisions and judgments called for in each of the questions.

\multicolumn{5}{c}{VACATION REQUESTS FOR THE ONE YEAR PERIOD FROM MAY 1, YEAR X THROUGH APRIL 30, YEAR Y}
Name	Work Assignment	Date Appointed	Accumulated Annual Leave Days	Vacation Periods Requested
DeMarco	MVO	Mar. 2003	25	May 3-21; Oct. 25-Nov. 5
Moore	Dispatcher	Dec. 1997	32	May 24-June 4; July 12-16
Kingston	MVO	Apr. 2007	28	May 24-June 11; Feb. 7-25
Green	MVO	June 2006	26	June 7-18; Sept. 6-24
Robinson	MVO	July 2008	30	June 28-July 9; Nov. 15-26
Reilly	MVO	Oct. 2009	23	July 5-9; Jan. 31-Mar. 3
Stevens	MVO	Sept. 1996	31	July 5-23; Oct. 4-29
Costello	MVO	Sept. 1998	31	July 5-30; Oct. 4-22
Maloney	Dispatcher	Aug. 1992	35	July 5-Aug. 6; Nov. 1-5
Hughes	Director	Feb. 1990	38	July 26-Sept. 3
Lord	MVO	Jan. 2010	20	Aug. 9-27; Feb. 7-25
Diaz	MVO	Dec. 2009	28	Aug. 9-Sept. 10
Krimsky	MVO	May 2006	22	Oct. 18-22: Nov. 22-Dec. 10

RULES AND GUIDELINES

1. The two Dispatchers cannot be on vacation at the same time, nor can a Dispatcher be on vacation at the same time as the Director.

2. For the period June 1 through September 30, not more than three MVO's can be on vacation at the same time.

3. For the period October 1 through May 31, not more than two MVO's at a time can be on vacation.

4. In cases where the same vacation time is requested by too many employees for all of them to be given the time under the rules, the requests of those who have worked the longest will be granted.

5. No employee may take more leave days than the number of annual leave days accumulated and shown in the table.

6. All vacation periods shown in the table and described in the questions below begin on a Monday and end on a Friday.

7. Employees work a five-day week (Monday through Friday). They are off weekends and holidays with no charges to leave balances. When a holiday falls on a Saturday or Sunday, employees are given the following Monday off without charge to annual leave.

8. Holidays: May 31   October 25   January 1
              July 4   November 2   February 12
              September 6 November 25   February 21
              October 11   December 25   February 21

9. An employee shall be given any part of his initial requests that is permissible under the above rules and shall have first right to it despite any further adjustment of schedule.

---

1. Until adjustments in the vacation schedule can be made, the vacation dates that can be approved for Krimsky are

   A. Oct. 18-22; Nov. 22-Dec. 10
   B. Oct. 18-22; Nov. 29-Dec. 10
   C. Oct. 18-22 *only*
   D. Nov. 22-Dec. 10 *only*

2. Until adjustments in the vacation schedule can be made, the vacation dates that can be approved for Maloney are

   A. July 5-Aug. 6; Nov. 1-5
   B. July 5-23; Nov. 1-5
   C. July 5-9; Nov. 1-5
   D. Nov. 1-5 *only*

3. According to the table, Lord wants a vacation in August and another in February. Until adjustments in the vacation schedule can be made, he can be allowed to take _____ of the August vacation and _____ of the February vacation.

   A. all; none   B. all; almost half
   C. almost all; almost half   D. almost half; all

4. Costello cannot be given all the vacation he has requested because

   A. the MVO's who have more seniority than he has have requested time he wishes
   B. he does not have enough accumulated annual leave
   C. a dispatcher is applying for vacation at the same time as Costello
   D. there are five people who want vacation in July

5. According to the table, how many leave days will DeMarco be charged for his vacation from October 25 through November 5?

   A. 10   B. 9   C. 8   D. 7

6. How many leave days will Moore use if he uses the requested vacation allowable to him under the rules?

   A. 9   B. 10   C. 14   D. 15

KEY (CORRECT ANSWERS)

1. D
2. B
3. A
4. B
5. C
6. A

TEST 5

Questions 1-8.

DIRECTIONS: Questions 1 through 8 are to be answered SOLELY on the basis of Charts I, II, III, and IV. Assume that you are the supervisor of Operators R, S, T, U, V, W, and X, and it is your responsibility to schedule their lunch hours.

The charts each represent a possible scheduling of lunch hours during a lunch period from 11:30 - 2:00. An operator-hour is one hour of time spent by one operator. Each box on the chart represents one half-hour. The boxes marked L represent the time when each operator is scheduled to have her lunch hour. For example, in Chart I, next to Operator R, the boxes for 11:30 - 12:00 and 12:00 -12:30 are marked L. This means that Operator R is scheduled to have her lunch hour from 11:30 to 12:30.

I

	11:30-12:00	12:00-12:30	12:30-1:00	1:00-1:30	1:30-2:00
R	L	L			
S		L	L		
T		L	L		
U			L	L	
V			L	L	
W				L	L
X				L	L

II

	11:30-12:00	12:00-12:30	12:30-1:00	1:00-1:30	1:30-2:00
R				L	L
S		L	L		
T	L	L			
U		L	L		
V				L	L
W				L	L
X	L	L			

III

	11:30-12:00	12:00-12:30	12:30-1:00	1:00-1:30	1:30-2:00
R	L	L			
S				L	L
T	L	L			
U			L	L	
V	L	L			
W			L	L	
X			L	L	

IV

	11:30-12:00	12:00-12:30	12:30-1:00	1:00-1:30	1:30-2:00
R	L	L			
S	L	L			
T			L	L	
U			L	L	
V				L	L
W				L	L
X				L	L

1. If, under the schedule represented in Chart II, Operator R has her lunch hour changed to 12:30-1:30, that leaves how many operator-hours of phone coverage from 1:00-2:00?

    A. 2   B. 2 1/2   C. 3   D. 4 1/2

2. If Operator S asks you whether she and Operator T may have the same lunch hour, you could accommodate her by using the schedule in Chart

    A. I   B. II   C. III   D. IV

3. From past experience you know that the part of the lunch period when the phones are busiest is from 12:30-1:30. Which chart shows the BEST phone coverage from 12:30 to 1:30?

    A. I   B. II   C. III   D. IV

4. At least three operators have the same lunch hour according to Chart(s)

    A. II and III   B. II and IV
    C. III only   D. IV only

128

2 (#5)

5. Which chart would provide the POOREST phone coverage during the period 12:00-1:30, based on total number of operator-hours from 12:00 to 1:30?   5.____

   A. I   B. II   C. III   D. IV

6. Which chart would make it possible for U, W, and X to have the same lunch hour?   6.____

   A. I   B. II   C. III   D. IV

7. The portion of the lunch period during which the telephones are least busy is 11:30-12:30.   7.____
   Which chart is MOST likely to have been designed with that fact in mind?

   A. I   B. II   C. III   D. IV

8. Assume that you have decided to use Chart IV to schedule your operators' lunch hours on a specific day. Operator T asks you if she can have her lunch hour changed to 1:00-2:00.   8.____
   If you grant her request, how many operators will be working during the period 12:00 to 12:30?

   A. 1   B. 2   C. 4   D. 5

KEY (CORRECT ANSWERS)

1. D
2. A
3. B
4. A
5. A

6. C
7. C
8. D

TEST 6

Questions 1-13.

DIRECTIONS: Questions 1 through 13 consist of a statement. You are to indicate whether the statement is TRUE (T) or FALSE (F). *PRINT THE LETTER OF THE CORRECT ANSWER IN THE SPACE AT THE RIGHT.* Questions 1 through 13 are to be answered SOLELY on the basis of the information given in the table below.

DEPARTMENT OF FERRIES ATTENDANTS WORK ASSIGNMENT - JULY 2003					
Name	Year Employed	Ferry Assigned	Hours of Work	Lunch Period	Days Off
Adams	1999	Hudson	7 AM - 3 PM	11-12	Fri. and Sat.
Baker	1992	Monroe	7 AM - 3 PM	11-12	Sun. and Mon.
Gunn	1995	Troy	8 AM - 4 PM	12-1	Fri. and Sat.
Hahn	1989	Erie	9 AM - 5 PM	1-2	Sat. and Sun.
King	1998	Albany	7 AM - 3 PM	11-12	Sun. and Mon.
Nash	1993	Hudson	11 AM - 7 PM	3-4	Sun. and Mon.
Olive	2003	Fulton	10 AM - 6 PM	2-3	Sat. and Sun.
Queen	2002	Albany	11 AM - 7 PM	3-4	Fri. and Sat.
Rose	1990	Troy	11 AM - 7 PM	3-4	Sun. and Mon.
Smith	1991	Monroe	10 AM - 6 PM	2-3	Fri. and Sat.

1. The chart shows that there are only five (5) ferries being used. 1._____

2. The attendant who has been working the LONGEST time is Rose. 2._____

3. The Troy has one more attendant assigned to it than the Erie. 3._____

4. Two (2) attendants are assigned to work from 10 P.M. to 6 A.M. 4._____

5. According to the chart, no more than one attendant was hired in any year. 5._____

6. The NEWEST employee is Olive. 6._____

7. There are as many attendants on the 7 to 3 shift as on the 11 to 7 shift. 7._____

8. MOST of the attendants have their lunch either between 12 and 1 or 2 and 3. 8._____

9. All the employees work four (4) hours before they go to lunch. 9._____

10. On the Hudson, Adams goes to lunch when Nash reports to work. 10._____

11. All the attendants who work on the 7 to 3 shift are off on Saturday and Sunday. 11._____

12. All the attendants have either a Saturday or Sunday as one of their days off. 12._____

13. At least two (2) attendants are assigned to each ferry. 13._____

KEY (CORRECT ANSWERS)

1. F
2. F
3. T
4. F
5. T
6. T
7. T
8. F
9. T
10. T
11. F
12. T
13. F

SUPERVISION STUDY GUIDE

Social science has developed information about groups and leadership in general and supervisor-employee relationships in particular. Since organizational effectiveness is closely linked to the ability of supervisors to direct the activities of employees, these findings are important to executives everywhere.

IS A SUPERVISOR A LEADER?

First-line supervisors are found in all large business and government organizations. They are the men at the base of an organizational hierarchy. Decisions made by the head of the organization reach them through a network of intermediate positions. They are frequently referred to as part of the management team, but their duties seldom seem to support this description.

A supervisor of clerks, tax collectors, meat inspectors, or securities analysts is not charged with budget preparation. He cannot hire or fire the employees in his own unit on his say-so. He does not administer programs which require great planning, coordinating, or decision making.

Then what is he? He is the man who is directly in charge of a group of employees doing productive work for a business or government agency. If the work requires the use of machines, the men he supervises operate them. If the work requires the writing of reports, the men he supervises write them. He is expected to maintain a productive flow of work without creating problems which higher levels of management must solve. But is he a leader?

To carry out a specific part of an agency's mission, management creates a unit, staffs it with a group of employees and designates a supervisor to take charge of them. Management directs what this unit shall do, from time to time changes directions, and often indicates what the group should not do. Management presumably creates status for the supervisor by giving him more pay, a title, and special privileges.

Management asks a supervisor to get his workers to attain organizational goals, including the desired quantity and quality of production. Supposedly, he has authority to enable him to achieve this objective. Management at least assumes that by establishing the status of the supervisor's position, it has created sufficient authority to enable him to achieve these goals—not his goals, nor necessarily the group's, but management's goals.

In addition, supervision includes writing reports, keeping records of membership in a higher-level administrative group, industrial engineering, safety engineering, editorial duties, housekeeping duties, etc. The supervisor as a member of an organizational network, must be responsible to the changing demands of the management above him. At the same time, he must be responsive to the demands of the work group of which he is a member. He is placed in the difficult position of communicating and implementing new decisions, changed programs and revised production quotas for his work group, although he may have had little part in developing them.

It follows, then, that supervision has a special characteristic: achievement of goals, previously set by management, through the efforts of others. It is in this feature of the supervisor's job that we find the role of a leader in the sense of the following definition: *A leader is that person who <u>most</u> effectively influences group activities toward goal setting and goal achievements.*

This definition is broad. It covers both leaders in groups that come together voluntarily and in those brought together through a work assignment in a factory, store, or government agency. In the natural group, the authority necessary to attain goals is determined by the group membership and is granted by them. In the working group, it is apparent that the establishment of a supervisory position creates a predisposition on the part of employees to accept the authority of the occupant of that position. We cannot, however, assume that mere occupation confers authority sufficient to assure the accomplishment of an organization's goals.

Supervision is different, then, from leadership. The supervisor is expected to fulfill the role of leader but without obtaining a grant of authority from the group he supervises. The supervisor is expected to influence the group in the achieving of goals but is often handicapped by having little influence on the organizational process by which goals are set. The supervisor, because he works in an organizational setting, has the burdens of additional organizational duties and restrictions and requirements arising out of the fact that his position is subordinate to a hierarchy of higher-level supervisors. These differences between leadership and supervision are reflected in our definition: *Supervision is basically a leadership role, in a formal organization, which has as its objective the effective influencing of other employees.*

Even though these differences between supervision and leadership exist, a significant finding of experimenters in this field is that supervisors <u>must</u> be leaders to be successful.

The problem is: How can a supervisor exercise leadership in an organizational setting? We might say that the supervisor is expected to be a natural leader in a situation which does not come about naturally. His situation becomes really difficult in an organization which is more eager to make its supervisors into followers rather than leaders.

LEADERSHIP: NATURAL AND ORGANIZATIONAL

Leadership, in its usual sense of *natural* leadership, and supervision are not the same. In some cases, leadership embraces broader powers and functions than supervision; in other cases, supervision embraces more than leadership. This is true both because of the organization and technical aspects of the supervisor's job and because of the relatively freer setting and inherent authority of the natural leader.

The natural leader usually has much more authority and influence than the supervisor. Group members not only follow his command but prefer it that way. The employee, however, can appeal the supervisor's commands to his union or to the supervisor's superior or to the personnel office. These intercessors represent restrictions on the supervisor's power to lead.

The natural leader can gain greater membership involvement in the group's objectives, and he can change the objectives of the group. The supervisor can attempt to gain employee support only for management's objectives; he cannot set other objectives. In these instances leadership is broader than supervision.

The natural leader must depend upon whatever skills are available when seeking to attain objectives. The supervisor is trained in the administrative skills necessary to achieve management's goals. If he does not possess the requisite skills, however, he can call upon management's technicians.

A natural leader can maintain his leadership, in certain groups, merely by satisfying members' need for group affiliation. The supervisor must maintain his leadership by directing and organizing his group to achieve specific organizational goals set for him and his group by management. He must have a technical competence and a kind of coordinating ability which is not needed by many natural leaders.

A natural leader is responsible only to his group which grants him authority. The supervisor is responsible to management, which employs him, and also to the work group of which he is a member. The supervisor has the exceedingly difficult job of reconciling the demands of two groups frequently in conflict. He is often placed in the untenable position of trying to play two antagonistic roles. In the above instance, supervision is broader than leadership.

ORGANIZATIONAL INFLUENCES ON LEADERSHIP

The supervisor is both a product and a prisoner of the organization wherein we find him. The organization which creates the supervisor's position also obstructs, restricts, and channelizes the exercise of his duties. These influences extend beyond prescribed functional relationships to specific supervisory behavior. For example, even in a face-to-face situation involving one of his subordinates, the supervisor's actions are controlled to a great extent by his organization. His behavior must conform to the organization policy on human relations, rules which dictate personnel procedures, specific prohibitions governing conduct, the attitudes of his own superior, etc. He is not a free agent operating within the limits of his work group. His freedom of action is much more circumscribed than is generally admitted. The organizational influences which limit his leadership actions can be classified as structure, prescriptions, and proscriptions.

The organizational structure places each supervisor's position in context with other designated positions. It determines the relationships between his position and specific positions which impinge on his. The structure of the organization designates a certain position to which he looks for orders and information about his work. It gives a particular status to his position within a pattern of statuses from which he perceives that (1) certain positions are on a par, organizationally, with his, (2) other positions are subordinate, and (3) still others are superior.

The organizational structure determines those positions to which he should look for advice and assistance, and those positions to which he should give advice and assistance.

For instance, the organizational structure has predetermined that the supervisor of a clerical processing unit shall report to a supervisory position in a higher echelon. He shall have certain relationships with the supervisors of the work units which transmit work to and receive work from his unit. He shall discuss changes and clarification of procedures with certain staff units, such as organization and methods, cost accounting, and personnel. He shall consult supervisors of units which provide or receive special work assignments.

The organizational structure, however, establishes patterns other than those of the relationships of positions. These are the patterns of responsibility, authority, and expectations.

The supervisor is responsible for certain activities or results; he is presumably invested with the authority to achieve these. His set of authority and responsibility is interwoven with other sets to the end that all goals and functions of the organization are parceled out in small, manageable lots. This, of course, establishes a series of expectations: a single supervisor can perform his particular set of duties only upon the assumption that preceding or contiguous sets of duties have been, or are being carried out. At the same time, he is aware of the expectations of others that he will fulfill his functional role.

The structure of an organization establishes relationships between specified positions and specific expectations for these positions. The fact that these relationships and expectations are established is one thing; whether or not they are met is another.

PRESCRIPTIONS AND PROSCRIPTIONS

But let us return to the organizational influences which act to restrict the supervisor's exercise of leadership. These are the prescriptions and proscriptions generally in effect in all organizations, and those peculiar to a single organization. In brief these are the *thou shalt's* and the *thou shalt not's*.

Organizations not only prescribe certain duties for individual supervisory positions, they also prescribe specific methods and means of carrying out these duties and maintaining management-employee relations. These include rules, regulations, policy, and tradition. It does no good for the supervisor to say, *This seems to be the best way to handle such-and-such,* if the organization has established a routine for dealing with problems. For good or bad, there are rules that state that firings shall be executed in such a manner, accompanied by a certain notification; that training shall be conducted, and in this manner. Proscriptions are merely negative prescriptions; you may not discriminate against any employee because of politics or race; you shall not suspend any employee without following certain procedures and obtaining certain approvals.

Most of these prohibitions and rules apply to the area of interpersonal relations, precisely the area which is now arousing most interest on the part of administrators and managers. We have become concerned about the contrast between formally prescribed relationships and interpersonal relationships, and this brings us to the often discussed informal organization.

FORMAL AND INFORMAL ORGANIZATIONS

As we well know, the functions and activities of any organization are broken down into individual units of work called positions. Administrators must establish a pattern which will link these positions to each other and relate them to a system of authority and responsibility. Man-to-man are spelled out as plainly as possible for all to understand. Managers, then, build an official structure which we call the formal organization.

In these same organizations, employees react individually and in groups to institutionally determined roles. John, a worker, rides in the same carpool as Joe, a foreman. An unplanned communication develops. Harry, a machinist knows more about high-speed machining than his foreman or anyone else in his shop. An unofficial tool boss comes into being. Mary, who fought with Jane, is promoted over her. Jane now gives Mary's directions. A planned relationship fails to develop. The employees have built a structure which we call the informal organization.

Formal organization is a system of management-prescribed relations between positions in an organization.

Informal organization is a network of unofficial relations between people in an organization.

These definitions might lead us to the absurd conclusion that positions carry out formal activities and that employe4es spend their time in unofficial activities. We must recognize that organizational activities are in all cases carried out by people. The formal structure provides a needed framework within which interpersonal relations occur. What we call informal organization is the complex of normal, natural relations among employees. These personal relationships may be negative or positive. That is, they may impede or aid the achievement of organizational goals. For example, friendship between two supervisors greatly increases the probability of good cooperation and coordination between their sections. On the other hand, *buck passing* nullifies the formal structure by failure to meet a prescribed and expected responsibility.

It is improbable that an ideal organization exists where all activities are carried out in strict conformity to a formally prescribed pattern of functional roles. Informal organization arises because of the incompleteness and ambiguities in the network of formally prescribed relationships, or in response to the needs or inadequacies of supervisors or managers who hold prescribed functional roles in an organization. Many of these relationships are not prescribed by the organizational pattern; many cannot be prescribed; many should not be prescribed.

Management faces the problem of keeping the informal organization in harmony with the mission of the agency. One way to do this is to make sure that all employees have a clear understanding of and are sympathetic with that mission. The issuance of organizational charts, procedural manuals, and functional descriptions of the work to be done by divisions and sections helps communicate management's plans and goals. Issuances alone, of course, cannot do the whole job. They should be accompanied by oral discussion and explanation. Management must ensure that there is mutual understanding and acceptance of charts and procedures. More important is that management acquaint itself with the attitudes, activities, and peculiar brands of logic which govern the informal organization. Only through this type of knowledge can they and supervisors keep informal goals consistent with the agency mission.

SUPERVISION STATUS AND FUNCTIONAL ROLE

A well-established supervisor is respected by the employees who work with him. They defer to his wishes. It is clear that a superior-subordinate relationship has been established. That is, status of the supervisor has been established in relation to other employees of the same work group. This same supervisor gains the respect of employees when he behaves in as certain manner. He will be expected, generally, to follow the customs of the group in such matters as dress, recreation, and manner of speaking. The group has a set of expectations as to his behavior. His position is a functional role which carries with it a collection of rights and obligations.

The position of supervisor usually has a status distinct from the individual who occupies it: it is much like a position description which exists whether or not there is an incumbent. The status of a supervisory position is valued higher than that of an employee position both because of the functional role of leadership which is assigned to it and because of the status symbols of titles, rights, and privileges which go with it.

Social ranking, or status, is not simple because it involves both the position and the man. An individual may be ranked higher than others because of his education, social background, perceived leadership ability, or conformity to group customs and ideals. If such a man is ranked higher by the members of a work group than their supervisor, the supervisor's effectiveness may be seriously undermined.

If the organization does not build and reinforce a supervisor's status, his position can be undermined in a different way. This will happen when managers go around rather than through the supervisor or designate him as a straw boss, acting boss, or otherwise not a real boss.

Let us clarify this last point. A role, and corresponding status, establishes a set of expectations. Employees expect their supervisor to do certain things and to act in certain ways. They are prepared to respond to that expected behavior. When the supervisor's behavior does not conform to their expectations, they are surprised, confused, and ill-at-ease. It becomes necessary for them to resolve their confusion, if they can. They might do this by turning to one of their own members for leadership. If the confusion continues, or their attempted solutions are not satisfactory, they will probably become a poorly motivated, non-cohesive group which cannot function very well.

COMMUNICATION AND THE SUPERVISOR

In a recent survey, railroad workers reported that they rarely look to their supervisor for information about the company. This is startling, at least to us, because we ordinarily think of the supervisor as the link between management and worker. We expect the supervisor to be the prime source of information about the company. Actually, the railroad workers listed the supervisor next to last in the o5rder of their sources of information. Most surprising of all, the supervisors, themselves, stated that rumor and unofficial contacts were their principal sources of information. Here we see one of the reasons why supervisors may not be as effective as management desires.

The supervisor is not only being bypassed by his work group, he is being ignored, and his position weakened, by the very organization which is holding him responsible for the activities of his workers. If he is management's representative to the employee, then management has an obligation to keep him informed of its activities. This is necessary if he is to carry out his functions efficiently and maintain his leadership in the work group. The supervisor is expected to be a source of information; when he is not, his status is not clear, and employees are dissatisfied because he has not lived up to expectations.

By providing information to the supervisor to pass along to employees, we can strengthen his position as leader of the group, and increase satisfaction and cohesion within the group. Because he has more information than the other members, receives information sooner, and passes it along at the proper times, members turn to him as a source and also provide him with information in the hope of receiving some in return. From this, we can see an increase in group cohesiveness because:

- Employees are bound closer to their supervisor because he is *in the know*.
- There is less need to go outside the group for answers
- Employees will more quickly turn to the supervisor for enlightenment

The fact that he has the answers will also enhance the supervisor's standing in the eyes of his men. This increased status will serve to bolster his authority and control of the group and will probably result in improved morale and productivity.

The foregoing, of course, does not mean that all management information should be given out. There are obviously certain policy determinations and discussions which need not or cannot be transmitted to all supervisors. However, the supervisor must be kept as fully informed as possible so that he can answer questions when asked and can allay needless fears and anxieties. Further, the supervisor has the responsibility of encouraging employee questions and submissions of information. He must be able to present information to employees so that it is clearly understood and accepted. His attitude and manner should make it clear that he believes in what he is saying, that the information is necessary or desirable to the group, and that he is prepared to act on the basis of the information.

SUPERVISION AND JOB PERFORMANCE

The productivity of work groups is a product; employees' efforts are multiplied by the supervision they receive. Many investigators have analyzed this relationship and have discovered elements of supervision which differentiate high and low production groups. These researchers have identified certain types of supervisory practices which they classify as *employee-centered* and other types which they classify as *production centered*.

The difference between these two kinds of supervision lies not in specific practices but in the approach or orientation to supervision. The employee-centered supervisor directs most of his efforts toward increasing employee motivation. He is concerned more with realizing the potential energy of persons than with administrative and technological methods of increasing efficiency and productivity. He is the man who finds ways of causing employees to want to work harder with the same tools. These supervisors emphasize the personal relations between their employees and themselves.

Now, obviously, these pictures are overdrawn. No one supervisor has all the virtues of the ideal type of employee-centered supervisor. And, fortunately, no one supervisor has all the bad traits found in many production-centered supervisors. We should remember that the various practices that researchers have fond which distinguish these two kinds of supervision represent the many practices and methods of supervisors of all gradations between these extremes. We should be careful, too, of the implications of the labels attached to the two types. For instance, being production-centered is not necessarily bad, since the principal responsibility of any supervisor is maintaining the production level that is expected of his work group. Being employee-centered may not necessarily be good, if the only result is a happy, chuckling crew of loafers. To return to the researchers' findings, employee-centered supervisors:

- Recommend promotions, transfers, pay increases
- Inform men about what is happening in the company
- Keep men posted on how well they are doing
- Hear complaints and grievances sympathetically
- Speak up for subordinates

Production-centered supervisors, on the other hand, don't do those things. They check on employees more frequently, give more detailed and frequent instructions, don't give reasons for changes, and are more punitive when mistakes are made. Employee-centered supervisors were reported to contribute to high morale and high production, whereas production-centered supervision was associated with lower morale and less production.

More recent findings, however, show that the relationship between supervision and productivity is not this simple. Investigators now report that high production is more frequently associated with supervisory practices which combine employee-centered behavior with concern for production. (This concern is not the same, however, as anxiety about production, which is the hallmark of our production-centered supervisor.) Let us examine these apparently contradictory findings and the premises from which they are derived.

SUPERVISION AND MORALE

Why do supervisory activities cause high or low production? As the name implies, the activities of the employee-centered supervisor tend to relate him more closely and satisfactorily to his workers. The production-centered supervisor's practices tend to separate him from his group and to foster antagonism. An analysis of this difference may answer our question.

Earlier, we pointed out that the supervisor is a type of leader and that leadership is intimately related to the group in which it occurs We discover, now, that an employee-centered supervisor's primary activities are concerned with both his leadership and his group membership. Such a supervisor is a member of a group and occupies a leadership role in that group.

These facts are sometimes obscured when we speak of the supervisor as management's representative, or as the organizational link between management and the employee, or as the end of the chain of command. If we really want to understand what it is we expect of the supervisor, we must remember that he is the designated leader of a group of employees to whom he is bound by interaction and interdependence.

Most of his actions are aimed, consciously or unconsciously, at strengthening membership ties in the group. This includes both making members more conscious that he is a member of their group) and causing members to identify themselves more closely with the group. These ends are accomplished by:

- making the group more attractive to the worker: they find satisfaction of their needs for recognition, friendship, enjoyable work, etc.;
- maintaining open communication: employees can express their views and obtain information about the organization
- giving assistance: members can seek advice on personal problems as well as their work; and
- acting as a buffer between the group and management: he speaks up for his men and explains the reasons for management's decisions.

Such actions both strengthen group cohesiveness and solidarity and affirm the supervisor's leadership position in the group.

DEFINING MORALE

This brings us back to a point mentioned earlier. We had said that employee-centered supervisors contribute to high morale as well as to high production. But how can we explain units which have low morale and high productivity, or vice versa? Usually production and morale are considered separately, partly because they are measured against different criteria and partly because, in some instances, they seem to be independent of each other.

Some of this difficulty may stem from confusion over definitions of morale. Morale has been defined as, or measured by, absences from work, satisfaction with job or company, dissension among members of work groups, productivity, apathy or lack of interest, readiness to help others, and a general aura of happiness as rated by observers. Some of these criteria of morale are not subject to the influence of the supervisor, and some of them are not clearly related to productivity. Definitions like these invite findings of low morale coupled with high production.

Both productivity and morale can be influenced by environmental factors not under the control of group members or supervisors. Such things as plant layout, organizational structure and goals, lighting, ventilation, communications, and management planning may have an adverse or desirable effect.

We might resolve the dilemma by defining morale on the basis of our understanding of the supervisor as leader of a group; morale is the degree of satisfaction of group members with their leadership. In this light, the supervisor's employee-centered activities bear a clear relation to morale. His efforts to increase employee identification with the group and to strengthen his leadership lead to greater satisfaction with that leadership. By increasing group cohesiveness and by demonstrating that his influence and power can aid the group, he is able to enhance his leadership status and afford satisfaction to the group.

SUPERVISION, PRODUCTION, AND MORALE

There are factors within the organization itself which determine whether increased production is possible:

- Are production goals expressed in terms understandable to employees and are they realistic?
- Do supervisors responsible for production respect the agency mission and production goals?
- If employees do not know how to do the job well, does management provide a trainer—often the supervisor—who can teach efficient work methods?

There are other factors within the work group which determine whether increased production will be attained:

- Is leadership present which can bring about the desired level of production?
- Are production goals accepted by employees as reasonable and attainable?
- If group effort is involved, are members able to coordinate their efforts?

Research findings confirm the view that an employee-centered supervisor can achieve higher morale than a production-centered supervisor. Managers may well ask what is the relationship between this and production.

Supervision is production-oriented to the extent that it focuses attention on achieving organizational goals, and plans and devises methods for attaining them; it is employee-centered to the extent that it focuses attention on employee attitudes toward those goals, and plans and works toward maintenance of employee satisfaction.

High productivity and low morale result when a supervisor plans and organizes work efficiently but cannot achieve high membership satisfaction. Low production and high morale result when a supervisor, though keeping members satisfied with his leadership, either has not gained acceptance of organizational goals or does not have the technical competence to achieve them.

The relationship between supervision, morale, and productivity is an interdependent one, with the supervisor playing an integral role due to his ability to influence productivity and morale independently of each other.

A supervisor who can plan his work well has good technical knowledge, and who can install better production methods can raise production without necessarily increasing group satisfaction. On the other hand, a supervisor who can motivate his employees and keep them satisfied with his leadership can gain high production in spite of technical difficulties and environmental obstacles.

CLIMATE AND SUPERVISION

Climate, the intangible environment of an organization made up of attitudes, beliefs, and traditions, plays a large part in morale, productivity, and supervision. Usually when we speak of climate and its relationship to morale and productivity, we talk about the merits of *democratic* versus *authoritarian* climate. Employees seem to produce more and have higher morale in a democratic climate, whereas in an authoritarian climate, the reverse seems to be true or so the researchers tell us. We would do well to determine what these terms mean to supervision.

Perhaps most of our difficulty in understanding and applying these concepts comes from our emotional reactions to the words themselves. For example, authoritarian climate is usually painted as the very blackest kind of dictatorship. This is not surprising, because we are usually expected to believe that it is invariably bad. Conversely, democratic climate is drawn to make the driven snow look impure by comparison.

Now these descriptions are most probably true when we talk about our political processes, or town meetings, or freedom of speech. However, the same labels have been used by social scientists in other contexts and have also been applied to government and business organizations, without it, it seems, any recognition that the meanings and their social values may have changed somewhat

For example, these labels were used in experiments conducted in an informal classroom setting using 11-year-old boys as subjects. The descriptive labels applied to the climate of the setting as well as the type of leadership practiced. When these labels were transferred to a management setting, it seems that many presumed that they principally meant the king of leadership rather than climate. We can see that there is a great difference between the experimental and management settings and that leadership practices for one might be inappropriate for the other.

It is doubtful that formal work organizations can be anything but authoritarian, in that goals are set by management and a hierarchy exists through which decisions and orders from the top are transmitted downward. Organizations are authoritarian by structure and need; direction and control are placed in the hands of a few in order to gain fast and efficient decision making. Now this does not mean to describe a dictatorship. It is merely the recognition of the fact that direction of organizational affairs comes from above. It should be noted that leadership in some natural groups is, in this sense, authoritarian.

Granting that formal organizations have this kind of authoritarian leadership, can there be a democratic climate? Certainly there can be, but we would want to define and delimit this term. A more realistic meaning of democratic climate in organizations is the use of permissive and participatory methods in management-employee relations. That is, a mutual exchange of information and explanation with the granting of individual freedom within certain restricted and defined limits. However, it is not our purpose to debate the merits of authoritarianism versus democracy. We recognize that within the small work group there is a need for freedom from constraint and an increase in participation in order to achieve organizational goals within the framework of the organizational movement.

Another aspect of climate is best expressed by this familiar, and true, saying: actions speak louder than words. Of particular concern to us is this effect of management climate on the behavior of supervisors, particularly in employee-centered activities.

There have been reports of disappointment with efforts to make supervisors ore employee-centered. Managers state that, since research has shown ways of improving human relations, supervisors should begin to practice these methods. Usually a training course in human relations is established; and supervisors are given this training. Managers then sit back and wait for the expected improvements, only to find that there are none.

If we wish to produce changes in the supervisor's behavior, the climate must be made appropriate and rewarding to the changed behavior. This means that top-level attitudes and behavior cannot deny or contradict the change we are attempting to effect. Basic changes in organizational behavior cannot be made with any permanence, unless we provide an environment that is receptive to the changes and rewards those persons who do change.

IMPROVING SUPERVISION

Anyone who has read this far might expect to find *A Dozen Rules for Dealing With Employees* or *29 Steps to Supervisory Success*. We will not provide such a list.

Simple rules suffer from their simplicity. They ignore the complexities of human behavior. Reliance upon rules may cause supervisors to concentrate on superficial aspects of their relations with employees. It may preclude genuine understanding.

The supervisor who relies on a list of rules tends to think of people in mechanistic terms. In a certain situation, he uses *Rule No. 3*. Employees are not treated as thinking and feeling persons, but rather as figures in a formula: Rule 3 applied to employee X = Production.

Employees usually recognize mechanical manipulation and become dissatisfied and resentful. They lose faith in, and respect for, their supervisor, and this may be reflected in lower morale and productivity.

We do not mean that supervisors must become social science experts if they wish to improve. Reports of current research indicate that there are two major parts of their job which can be strengthened through self-improvement: (1) Work planning, including technical skills, and (2) motivation of employees.

The most effective supervisors combine excellence in the administrative and technical aspects of their work with friendly and considerate personal relations with their employees.

CRITICAL PERSONAL RELATIONS

Later in this chapter we shall talk about administrative aspects of supervision, but first let us comment on *friendly and considerate personal relations*. We have discussed this subject throughout the preceding chapters, but we want to review some of the critical supervisory influences on personal relations.

Closeness of Supervision: The closeness of supervision has an important effect on productivity and morale. Mann and Dent found that supervisors of low-producing units supervise very closely, while high-producing supervisors exercise only general supervision. It was found that the low-producing supervisors:

- check on employees more frequently
- give more detailed and frequent instructions
- limit employee's freedom to do job in own way

Workers who felt less closely supervised reported that they were better satisfied with their jobs and the company. We should note that the manner or attitude of the supervisor has an important bearing on whether employees perceive supervision as being close or general.

These findings are another way of saying that supervision does not mean standing over the employee and telling him what to do and when and how to do it. The more effective supervisor tells his employees what is required, giving general instructions.

COMMUNICATION

Supervisors of high-production units consider communication as one of the most important aspects of their job. Effective communication is used by these supervisors to achieve better interpersonal relations and improved employee motivation. Low-production supervisors do not rate communications as highly important.

High-producing supervisors find that an important aid to more effective communication is listening. They are ready to listen to both personal problems or interests and questions about the work. This does not mean that they are *nosey* or meddle in their employees' personal lives, but rather that they show a willingness to listen, and do listen, if their employees wish to discuss problems.

These supervisors inform employees about forthcoming changes in work; they discuss agency policy with employees; and they make sure that each employee knows how well he is doing. What these supervisors do is use two-way communication effectively. Unless the supervisor freely imparts information, he will not receive information in return.

Attitudes and perception are frequently affected by communication or the lack of it. Research surveys reveal that many supervisors are not aware of their employees' attitudes, nor do they know what personal reactions their supervision arouses. Through frank discussion with employees, they have been surprised to discover employee beliefs about which they were ignorant. Discussion sometimes reveals that the supervisor and his employees have totally different impressions about the same event. The supervisor should be constantly on the alert for misconceptions about his words and deeds. He must remember that, although his actions are perfectly clear to himself, they may be, and frequently are, viewed differently by employees.

Failure to communicate information results in misconceptions and false assumptions. What you say and how you say it will strongly affect your employees' attitudes and perceptions. By giving them available information, you can prevent misconceptions; by discussion, you may be able to change attitudes; by questioning, you can discover what the perceptions and assumptions really are. And it need hardly be added that actions should conform very closely to words.

If we were to attempt to reduce the above discussion on communication to rules, we would have a long list which would be based on one cardinal principle: Don't make assumptions!

- Don't assume that your employees know; tell them.
- Don't assume that you know how they feel; find out.
- Don't assume that they understand; clarify.

20 SUPERVISORY HINTS

1. Avoid inconsistency.
2. Always give employees a chance to explain their action before taking disciplinary action. Don't allow too much time for a "cooling off" period before disciplining an employee.
3. Be specific in your criticisms.
4. Delegate responsibility wisely.
5. Do not argue or lose your temper, and avoid being impatient.
6. Promote mutual respect and be fair, impartial, and open-minded.
7. Keep in mind that asking for employees' advice and input can be helpful in decision making.
8. If you make promises, keep them.
9. Always keep the feelings, abilities, dignity and motives of your staff in mind.
10. Remain loyal to your employees' interests.
11. Never criticize employees in front of others, or treat employees like children.
12. Admit mistakes. Don't place blame on your employees, or make excuses.
13. Be reasonable in your expectations, give complete instructions, and establish well-planned goals.
14. Be knowledgeable about office details and procedures, but avoid becoming bogged down in details.
15. Avoid supervising too closely or too loosely. Employees should also view you as an approachable supervisor.
16. Remember that employees' personal problems may affect job performance, but become involved only when appropriate.
17. Work to develop workers, and to instill a feeling of cooperation while working toward mutual goals.
18. Do not overpraise or underpraise, be properly appreciative.
19. Never ask an employee to discipline someone for you.
20. A complaint, even if unjustified, should be taken seriously.

NOTES